T0123746

Not Wasting a Save

A Journey of Finding Faith

JOY SCHULZ

WestBow Press books may be ordered through booksellers or by contacting:

WestBow Press
A Division of Thomas Nelson & Zondervan
1663 Liberty Drive
Bloomington, IN 47403
www.westbowpress.com
1 (866) 928-1240

Interior Image Credit: David Schulz Photography (Heron)

ISBN: 978-1-9736-8645-3 (sc)
ISBN: 978-1-9736-8644-6 (e)

Print information available on the last page.

WestBow Press rev. date: 03/03/2020

ACKNOWLEDGEMENTS

This book is dedicated to the many angels who have walked beside me on the mountaintop highs, stood beside me in the valley lows, and to all who have inspired me along the way. And a special thank you to my family for giving me the time to follow my dreams of finding happiness and finding my faith. But most of all, thank you to my Father in Heaven who has guided me through my many detours, picked me up countless times, who fought for me and never left my side.

This is for you.

CONTENTS

Introduction ix

Part I Finding Faith

Chapter 1 Do you believe in luck? 1
Chapter 2 Finding faith in a sea of purple. 13
Chapter 3 Sometimes we stumble. 23

Part II Hope

Chapter 4 What it means to hope. 29
Chapter 5 H is for healing. 31
Chapter 6 O is for optimism. 35
Chapter 7 P is for perseverance. 39
Chapter 8 E is for endurance. 45

Part III Raw Faith

Chapter 9 What if life is not about you? 51
Chapter 10 How do you get raw faith? 55
Chapter 11 The surrendering begins. 63
Chapter 12 How deep is your faith? 69

Part IV Perseverance

Chapter 13 Run like you mean it. 75
Chapter 14 Angels in our midst. 81

Chapter 15 Running a marathon is facing a giant. 85
Chapter 16 Big things come in small packages. 93

Part V Free Will

Chapter 17 You are the light of the world. 99
Chapter 18 What's your word? 103
Chapter 19 Don't let fear win. 109
Chapter 20 The gift of opportunity. 117

Part VI Grace

Chapter 21 Are grace and mercy the same? 123
Chapter 22 Making a timeline. 125
Chapter 23 Dare you to move. 127
Chapter 24 Following your dreams. 133

Part VII Prayer

Chapter 25 The power behind prayer. 139
Chapter 26 Forgiveness is hard. 147

Part VIII Understanding

Chapter 27 Expect the unexpected. 153
Chapter 28 What's it going to be? 157
Chapter 29 Are you a strategic planner? 159

Part IX Blessed

Chapter 30 Sitting in it. 169

INTRODUCTION

Here it is: a look back on my journey of the twists and turns that have led me to where I am today. Sitting here anxious about exposing it all—how God has chased me down, intercepted on my behalf, and how His grace has led me to this very spot, this place of kneeling before the cross—is a little difficult for me. To reveal in these moments that my life is not perfect, that I don't have it all together, and that sometimes you have to walk away from the closed doors, is a humbling prospect. But one that's hopefully worth sharing.

This journey has included many of the finest of moments that I would never trade, whether I noticed at the time or not. When things are going well, we remain on autopilot and don't give much thought to the how's and why's of our good fortune. You may not even think that God is intercepting on a daily basis on your behalf or fully comprehend that His love is greater than anything you could ever imagine. These interceptions, or what I call detours, are intended to get us back on track. They're second chances or life savers, in my case. I reflect back on how many times things didn't go my way and how disappointed I was in not getting the answers I thought I needed. But now, years later, I recognize that those disappointments were best for me, that the detour given was a better way.

This book is about those detours, road blocks, and lifesaving moments, which led me on my journey to the cross in finding my faith. He has shown great mercy, given much grace, and extended me supernatural patience. It's taken forty-plus years to get my footing on solid ground and striving to "get it right." This I do know: When my heavenly Father calls me home, upon entering the pearly gates, the words I want to hear are "Joy, it was a rough start but you finished strong, job well done!" That is why I'm here, this "call out" to be humble and to extend my faith to others in order to help them on their path. It's called "giving your testimony" in sharing your faith and your journey. By sharing one's life and faith—the good, the bad, and the ugly—it can bolster the faith of someone else. To not share what God has done for me would be "wasting a save," many saves, in His efforts to chase me down and the countless moments of Him carrying me through each and every one of them. We will also follow people of the Bible whose lives, in certain situations, often parallel our own. We share a common struggle with doubt, fear and detours in our faith, when it's difficult to just trust God's intentions for our lives.

I hope that you can be honest with yourself and relate to the similarities between life's worries and fears of these biblical characters with your own. The goal of this book is to communicate that life is not perfect, situations happen, wrong choices are made, but through all of them, there is hope that each day offers a new start. As in Lamentations 3:22-23, "The steadfast love of the Lord never ceases; His mercies never come to an end; they are new every morning; great is Your faithfulness." I hope that as you engage with my journey and those of the bible, you connect with God on a deeper level and discover *your* true faith. I pray that you recognize the nudges or little moments of grace that would otherwise go unnoticed and acknowledge Him in a way that is different than before.

God gives us hope to strengthen our faith, to believe in the unseen—and that, my friend, is where changes in your life begin. It changes our very existence here on earth—or at least it did in mine. I hope you find and experience hope through my journey, through my testimony and *believe* in His mercy and *accept* His grace when given. Acceptance is the first step in believing that His plan is for good no matter what happens, no matter what the circumstances are. That's hard to say and I have to repeat it every day to remind myself of this great love. So here it is…this is me not wasting a save. It's a few of my situations, my wrong and right choices and everything in between… where He saved me on my journey to the cross. So walk with me, friend; I want to share with you this great love that is here and introduce you to a Father who walks with you daily. Take my hand, let's go.

Finding Faith

He replied, "Because you have so little faith. Truly I tell you, if you have faith as small as a mustard seed, you can say to this mountain, 'Move from here to there,' and it will move. Nothing will be impossible for you."
~ Matthew 17:20

CHAPTER 1

Do you believe in luck?

Why is it that when things are going well in our lives, we call it luck or good fortune? Growing up, I never considered God's presence in my life. I grew up in a home where God was never really talked about, nor did we attend church. The thought of God was that He was a holy man in a white robe up in Heaven who judged my every move. I believed that He was only present in my failures, in giving "the look."

You know the look. Like the one your parents give you when you've done something stupid. I expected only disappointment from Him throughout my childhood, and never recognized Him as playing an active role in my daily life. My perception of God's view of my life could be summed up by, "Nice try, better luck next time." I'd like to think I had some bright moments that pleased Him, but mostly they were characterized by a never-ending search for happiness outside of Him. Happiness which I'd been told was just around the corner, but seemed elusive to me. I aspired to be a good person, knew right from wrong, was kind to others and wanted to do the right thing—most of the time. Having been on autopilot for the first forty years was altogether exhausting, as if I was in control of every moment of my life. To be in control would mean that I was acting as my own kind of god and what I did and accomplished was all my own doing. As if! And why is it that when there are those valley-moments, in the trenches, those low moments where

[We are refined in the valleys.]

all you can do is cry out to God "Why?" you question your faith and His existence? As though suddenly you're *not* the one in control and you blame God for everything that's happened. You ask questions, such as "Is He for real? Is Heaven for real? Does He really love me?" You say to yourself, "If God has allowed this to happen in my life, maybe He doesn't love me or care." We question our beliefs and our faith is tested in those valley-moments where we waver on the edge of uncertainty.

We teeter on the precipice of what I call *empty faith*, the kind that never fully develops and we find our life unsatisfying and altogether empty. We do not realize that it is in those teaching moments and in those valleys where we are refined, tested and given strength way beyond what we deserve. We learn about defeat, heartache, and it is in those depths that we learn about ourselves and how far we can go.

[*He walks with us through it.*]

It is in this doubt where your faith strengthens and God shows patience with those who seek Him. It is in the doubting that we recognize our relationship through conversations as a child is with a father. It is through His mercy and grace that He gives us new days, new chances to find our way, to discover the strength, courage and will needed to survive it. This is where we strengthen our hearts for the next leg of our journey and remember that God represents love and *IS* love.

But sometimes that's a hard one to swallow. I sometimes choke on that one and wonder, if we love Him and He loves us, then why is it when there is pain and turmoil in our lives, a real doubt comes into the picture and we start to question everything.

I was asked to join a bible study about contentment. That's funny because I'm way too busy, right? My goal this year was to accept opportunities that move me forward, so I found myself in the middle of the desert with the Israelites complaining about everything. The study was about finding contentment in where God has you in every season of your life. It doesn't mean that you will stay there but trusting His choices for you, in every moment, is where the struggle comes in. I connected with the Israelites in their constant chatter and list of complaints and could relate in their dissatisfaction. Have you ever experienced a turn of events that elicits more things to complain about? The Israelites wandered in the desert for forty years in hopes of reaching the Promise Land and grumbled the entire time. As I went through the study, I scoffed at their whining about everything and thought, "Well, I never would have..." Oh, but I have. As I write this, I feel as if I've been in the desert and have done nothing but complain. I have days where I see God's hand and then the next day, I find reasons to be dissatisfied and begin to grumble.

Questions for Your Journey

- Can you recall a situation where you complained about something that you couldn't see beyond? Did you complain to others and notice that the mood changed and your grumbling was contagious?

- List one thing you are grateful for.

Complaining is a bad habit and it is also very contagious. It happens in a group of people and before you know it, everyone is jumping in. In order to break this habit, during the study we were given a "contentment bracelet." Every time you complained you were to move the bracelet to the other wrist and think of something for which you were grateful. I have to admit, there were days in the beginning where I wore that bracelet out; all the wrist changing was overwhelming. But as I continued this process, I began to recognize all the things I was grateful for and realized it was much easier to focus on the good things. Then it became easier to demonstrate grace to those around me.

I started this with one of my sons who complains more than he should. Once he recognized his habit of being dissatisfied, he began appreciating the people and things around him as I challenged him to find the good. It's all in the "eyes wide open" moments and praising God for them. I was becoming more content in my own life as I followed along in the Israelites journey, which, because of their grumbling took forty years instead of the eleven days it was supposed to! I encourage you to read Numbers to gain a greater grasp of what God's grace really means. Stop complaining and be grateful.

So do you believe in luck? I view luck a little differently now. By living most of my life dependent on luck, waiting for good things to happen, I was at the mercy of whimsy, just hoping to get it right. Leaning on luck relegates your success to chance or good fortune, rather than the impact of your own abilities. It perpetuates the fallacy that you don't have to take an active role in your success, but just hope you'll get lucky and something good will happen. How many times do we say, "Good luck!" to someone, as if they don't have the ability to succeed without it? We're essentially saying they have no control over their own success, but are at the mercy of luck and chance.

But what about when you are in a valley moment and all you care about is what YOU are going through and you simply hope for luck. Does God have anything to do with luck? God does not promise us a life free from failure, pain, or loss. But the beauty in a relationship with Him is recognizing that whatever the situation, He walks with us through it, never leaving our side. When I think about moments in my life where the pain was real, I used to feel so alone. But the images of what I see now are Him curled up on the floor with me when I didn't have the strength to stand, or His stride running through the rain, wiping my tears when I couldn't see through the pain. These images are what get me through the day. It's all in the conversation with Him, embracing the true love that He has for us that is given so freely, that is the real deal. It's in truly understanding that we will never be alone, even when we fall.

So why is it so hard to love without conditions? I believe that love *is* based on conditions, or at least expectations we hold each other to. As much as I want to say that I love my husband or family without conditions, it would be a lie. Yes, I love them. Yes, I care about them. But it is all based on a mutual expectation that we have of both people giving and receiving love. To know love—the real stuff, the God love—is to know that it is infallible and there are no conditions or restrictions to it. The closest human comparison to His unconditional love is the love I have for my children.

[*He still hasn't changed His mind in loving you.*]

To be open to love we need the ability to love freely, fundamentally, and unconditionally like Christ. I have to remind myself that all the rest is Satan and the games he plays to evoke fear and doubt. He steers us away from ever having a complete and trusting relationship. So then we play the blame game. We forget that just maybe we played a leading role in this turmoil, that quite possibly *we* made the decisions that led us to where we find ourselves. I know I have, many times; too many to count. Yet God still hasn't changed His mind about me, in loving me.

Questions for Your Journey

- Recall a time when you played a leading role in a decision made by you that probably was not the best. What was your detour that God gave you to get you back on track?

- Do you think luck has anything to do with contentment?

This reminds me of a story of a man named Thomas who allowed doubt to set in and block his path to belief. I can relate and mirror that same doubt in my life.

In setting the scene in John 20:24-29, Thomas had not been with the disciples when they had seen Jesus after the resurrection. They told Thomas, but he still doubted that they even saw him at all and stated that the only way he would believe was by seeing Jesus for himself. How many times do we put such restrictions in the *just believing* part of this thing called faith? We have a list in order for us to feel at ease in the unseen. In this same way, Thomas continued to doubt. When Jesus reappeared to the disciples once again, Thomas saw him. Knowing of his doubt, Jesus then turned and addressed Thomas, while holding up his hands to show him the nail holes. He told him to believe. It is in that moment that doubt flees and Thomas believes. I too often put such restrictions on believing God's existence by asking for miracles or demanding proof that He is really there. Sometimes He humors us with those brief moments of what we call "that was weird." But, whether it was a moment of decline in what we wanted, or a moment of giving in to what we never thought would happen, these are the instances of truth where faith takes shape. Call them detours or call them fate, either way they are His calls, not ours to make.

Questions for Your Journey

- ❖ Have you ever had a "that was a weird kind of moment?" Write it down.

- ❖ Have you taken a detour or did you jump in and go on faith? What was the outcome?

But sometimes those detours are no fault of our own. Things happen in our lives that are not always a result of any decision we made, but one made for us, for various reasons. Sometimes in our lives things happen, such as diagnosis, career change, or betrayal that is beyond our control. I do not take this lightly and I am not saying that God instigates a devastating diagnosis or any other unpleasant situation caused by another. Please hear me when I say this. I have suffered from a few and I get it. I have had choices made for me by the actions of someone else or through no fault of my own. But it was within those moments that I had to move forward and decide what to do with it. My choices at that crossroads determined the outcome of my future. Do we grow from it or do we stand still and continue to live in it? Do we let it steal our joy, compromise our future or do we push through it and press on? We all have choices and each choice has led us to where we are right now; so what are you going to do with it?

I heard a sermon once that we have participated in every good or bad decision in our lives—a true statement. An example of not having a say in an outcome in my life is that I've had health issues for over twenty-five years and most days are a struggle. Few people know this about me because I am out there running, biking and appear healthy on the outside, but in reality, it's a life of discipline and restrictions daily. There are days that I wish for a meal pill that I could take instead. I'm sick most of the time but by watching what I eat, I am able to somewhat control the outcome of my day. That is where discipline comes in.

With this health struggle, I find comfort in Hebrews 12:11. It reads, "No discipline seems pleasant at the time, but painful. Later on, however, it produces a harvest of righteousness and peace for those who have been trained by it." In living with discipline for so long, I insert and create opportunities now that require me to have discipline. In thriving in it and moving me forward in keeping me close in knowing and having the understanding of my strengths and weaknesses. I literally eat the same thing every day. I don't wander too far, and if I do, my gut will let me know about it. But it is within this discipline that I became more aware of life around me and that is where my focus on finding my faith began.

Questions for Your Journey

- ❖ Is there an area in your life that requires you to be more disciplined? How are you handling it?

- ❖ What are three steps that you could insert into your daily routine to become more disciplined?

I have had many bouts with pre-cancer but never much further than that because the word "pre" in front of anything makes you feel as if you have been given a chance. But I *have* had experience in the realm of cancer. I've had family, friends, and people I don't even know hear those words and I pray for them daily.

I had the privilege of working with the American Cancer Society for several years, and it was within those years where my faith actually grew. It was in those moments of deep valleys where I began to understand this blind faith and what that means. It was in those face-to-face moments of walking alongside many who were in that valley where I began *finding my faith.*

CHAPTER 2

Finding faith in a sea of purple.

One of the first memories for me in experiencing true faith was in a sea of purple. This is where the true meaning of "strength in numbers" came alive for me. A very good friend of mine was diagnosed with breast cancer and introduced me to the world of a *Relay for Life* event. I was in awe of her strength, determination, and will to survive as I watched her lead, inspire, and change the lives of those around her while also going through the same diagnosis. But upon entering my first Relay for Life event, I experienced something I never thought would be so transformational while witnessing the depths of so much darkness. To witness a great love of friends and family in just one lap was life-changing for me. I knew in that instant that I was now part of something so much bigger than me and it had nothing to do with me. It was in that moment where I stepped out of my life, my problems, and my moments of selfishness and realized what it meant to love others for no other reason than to just walk alongside them. As that year turned into now 15 years of relaying, I continued in this fight with these individuals who inspired me. This is where I witnessed true faith that persevered through the

> [*Find faith in the valley moments.*]

trenches no matter what, no matter the outcome. It was through witnessing a survivor's faith that my faith exploded.

In speaking of faith and giants, this brings me to the story of David and Goliath. How many of us have a story like this! How many times did something so big stand in your way of greatness, taunting you like a giant? What inspires me the most in this story is that against all odds, the faith of David was larger than any situation or circumstance that most would run from. I think of this story often in my life, and then I gather my stones and just go on faith. It sounds easy, but most times I stick those stones in my pocket and save them for a rainy day. I feel I have been running my entire life and in just the last few years I've taken those stones out of my pocket and have just gone on faith.

Questions for Your Journey

- ❖ Can you remember a time when you experienced a deeper level of faith just by witnessing someone else's faith?

- ❖ What do you do when faced with a giant? Do you go on fear or do you lean on faith?

To set the stage of this great warrior, in 1 Samuel 17, David was the youngest of eight sons of Jesse from Bethlehem in Judah. David's position in the family was to look after his father's sheep while his three older brothers went to war against the Philistines under the ruling of Saul. Among the Philistines there was a man named Goliath who was said to have been six cubits and a span (that's nine feet and six inches!). He challenged the Israelites, shouting out to Saul's men to fight him and if they were able to kill him, then the Philistines would then have to serve the Israelites. But if Goliath killed the challenger, then the Israelites would then have to serve the Philistines. It was David's job to take grain and bread to his brothers in battle, and it was there that he heard the demands of Goliath. He watched as those around him ran in fear, retreating from the thought of defeat and death. With his faith in tow, David picked up five smooth stones and put them in his pocket and challenged the giant through his enormous faith in proclaiming the name of his Lord. It was through his faith in a God who he knew was with him, and believing that with his whole heart, that he won. Starting in verse 34 we see David's faith was strong, and that Saul believed and suited him for war. It was with this faith that he faced down the fear and overtook evil, giving praise to the one and only God. Isn't life like this that we all have our own giants and obstacles that take over our lives?

It is by faith that you can stare down fear by proclaiming the name of the Lord.

We all have fears that stop us in our tracks and we turn and run the other way, just as the Israelites did. We leave our victories on the path and we stand still in fear, never taking a forward step. If only we could all take the wooden staff of faith and break those barriers which we create and break through to the glory of what God has in store for us, just on the other side of fear. It's as simple as five smooth stones and a whole lot of faith, and victory is ours to claim. When reading this, I found that the number five has very significant meaning in the Bible:

- The number five symbolizes God's *grace*.
- The number five is recited 318 times in the bible.

- The Ten Commandments have two sets of five.
- There are five sections in the book of Psalms.
- There are five books of law. (Genesis, Exodus, Leviticus, Numbers, Deuteronomy)
- The apostle Paul wrote five books.
- Jesus multiplied five loaves to feed 5,000.
- In Exodus, the tabernacle was made of five curtains, five bars, five pillars, five sockets and an altar made of five cubits wide and five cubits long. The height of the court in the tabernacle is five cubits.
- The holy anointing oils were made of five parts, with all the spices being measured out in multiples of five.
- Moses wrote five books.

There are many other references to the number five that are relevant. In studying the word "smooth," as in the stones being smooth, what I found is this. When tested, tried and true, you are bound to end up with smooth stones that have weathered the storms. And it is within the imagery of these smooth stones where our faith has been tested in the rough waters of life and we have grown wiser and stronger. God is within the spirit of these stones and can do great things by coming to our rescue in the just believing part. It is in these battles with giants that we can retreat or move forward with the power of the Lord, and that, my friend is where our battles are won.

It is the gathering of stones and our faith that life changes.

Questions for Your Journey

- ❖ What is a Goliath moment that you need to take out your stones you've been holding in your pocket that you need to launch in the way of fear?

- ❖ List one fear that stops you in your tracks in pursuing a victory.

FIVE

F = Faith **I** = Is **V** = Victorious **E** = Every time

That is what I saw during my time at ACS when faced with a Goliath—strength that seemed impossible. I saw the hand of God on individuals where His light shone through every aspect of their life, their families and in those around them. My time there was one of the most rewarding times of my life, but also one of the hardest. I have to admit; it tested my faith many times over, asking the question "why" these people have to suffer, and it broke my heart. In those moments of looking into the eyes of a mother as her child is fitted for a wig, it was all I could do to hold it together. I would imagine the overwhelming strength it must have taken to stand in those moments, facing those odds, yet somehow moving forward as a mom-warrior, sounded unimaginable to me. I would go to my office and cry; just cry and pray I could give my strength to that mom that day and to the child in the fight of their lives. In the communities I visited daily, I had the opportunity to just listen to their stories about themselves or their loved ones and was astounded. They believed, against all odds, they had the power to survive and demonstrated an unshakable faith, a "never give up" attitude. A gentleman in treatment once told me, alongside his wife also in treatment, that the moment the doctors tell you that you have so many months to live is *the very exact and precise moment in which you want to live the most.* It's where your past and your future collide and nothing is more important than the present. It is the same exact moment where all your dreams come rushing in and the overwhelming sense of urgency to do and say everything that you always wished for now has a deadline. I was in awe and admiration of their testimonies and their faith being confident that God was walking beside them and in control. Those moments often were the most peaceful, as though they had lent me their faith, just to have a taste of what true faith was really like. What's there to lose with a fatal diagnosis; why not put it all on the line and take a leap of faith? Going all in, fearless and having no regrets. Surly there is a time in your life that you were against all odds where you may have felt that same feeling; Where you teetered on the edge of the cliff of faith, but you pushed off and allowed the presence of God to take over. That the one decision you were to make was somehow going to be the answer to everything.

It is in those moments where you have to go on gut and be willing to allow God to just be God. It was in those moments I began to see God's mercy that helped to strengthen my faith in believing that He is, was and always will be present, no matter how ugly the situation is, no matter how dark the room is; He is light. It is only through His love and grace where He shines in darkness, and where He brings life to any situation.

And then it happened—where my faith was present in what I call a moment of knee buckling. This past year only a few weeks apart, my mother and mother-in-law were both diagnosed with cancer. The questioning, the doubts came flooding in; the walking alongside these great warriors, their stories, their faith brought me to my knees in prayer. But that was the place I needed to be. I imagined them standing beside me in this moment encouraging me to look up. The humbling of ourselves amidst tragic times remind us who is in control and who is present. In preparing me for this moment of doubt, He reminded me of my past of walking beside His greatest warriors, the ones who lent me their faith, now who came rushing in to deliver me from my doubt. To believe in the one and only Father who prepares your path and prepared my path for me in this very moment. He prepares your path each day by giving you experiences and moments *for* your future. In walking you through those valleys He's preparing you for what's up ahead, for in the "what's next."

[*He prepares your path for moments in your future.*]

What's beautiful about this raw faith though is that you accept His plan and His will and you understand that whatever may come, you know He will be in it. And it is in this raw place that you not only begin to live in such a way *through* your faith but ***on*** your faith; on solid ground.

Questions for Your Journey

- Describe a time where you let God take the wheel.

- Recall a time in your life when God prepared you ahead of time for that moment where your faith was solid. Praise God!

CHAPTER 3

Sometimes we stumble.

So now that you know where I began finding my faith, this brings me to a time in which I had lost all faith, questioned His existence, and felt as if I'd become the main character in this horror flick. This was way before my newfound faith and I was swimming in the depths of what I thought was my very own existence. I am not proud to say that I withdrew and found myself alone, never turning to God, never seeking Him, or acknowledging Him in the room.

"Everything is temporary" is a phrase that I tell myself. During darkness we have to believe that it's not the end and believe that this too shall pass. But I can say that while in the moment of feeling that gut-wrenching pain, all you want is out. Looking for any way to escape, the fastest and easiest way is typically the path most traveled, isn't it? It's the path the enemy lays out before us and promises us quick results with much less effort on our part. It's the moments that whatever the cost, it doesn't matter, just make it quick. So when we're looking back on the moments where our valleys were deep, God finds us and always extends a hand. He lifts us up and sets us back on the path to move us forward. And the funny thing is that we don't even realize it. All day, every minute, every second He is working on your behalf. How many times have you gotten through a situation and you felt like things just turned around? It's a miracle, right?

God finds us and always extends a hand.

Good fortune or even yet, luck. But it was on this day I saw a speck; it was just a seed planted that maybe, just maybe He was there. It was on this journey to the cross where I found my strength, my hope, and my everlasting God. And it was within this horror flick in which hope took on another meaning. It was where that seed took root and I wasn't lost at all. It all started with something that resembled a glimmer of hope.

Questions for Your Journey

- ❖ Was there a time in your life where you doubted God?

- ❖ What does faith mean to you?

Hope

"For I know the plans I have for you." Declares the Lord, "Plans to prosper you and not to harm you, plans to give you *hope* and a future."
~ Jeremiah 29:11

CHAPTER 4

What it means to hope.

Hope is a big word, although it has only four letters. We use it all the time as if having hope is the answer when we have nothing else to look forward to; nothing to count on, nothing to lose. Hope is what God gives us in those valleys in helping to lead us back up the mountain. Some call it a lifeline; I call it courage to believe in something beyond oneself. It is in getting us there, to the top, where hope gives meaning to the chaos you've just experienced, but without those valleys we are unable to grow for whatever His plan is for us. It is in those valleys where we learn from it and experience life, where it truly makes a difference in how we move forward.

There are many Scriptures on hope that give meaning to the word. In Jeremiah 29:11, "For I know the plans I have for you, declares the Lord, plans to prosper you and not to harm you, plan to give you ***hope*** and a future." God gives us hope by pulling us along through the muck of despair on our journey called life. His plan is to give us hope and that's good news to me! In searching for more info about the word hope, I found that it can either be used as a verb or a noun. This is the part where my teacher comes out, so just go with it and let's learn.

Its origin of first use was before the twelfth century, meaning before the year 1101. It's been around a long time and yet we still have trouble with it. The verb form of the word defined is "to expect with confidence or to trust." In noun form, its meaning would also be "trust or rely on expecting fulfillment." According to Merriam Webster, "*hope*, *expect* and *look* all mean to await some occurrence or outcome." To *expect* implies a high degree of certainty and usually involves the idea of preparing or envisioning. This is where we expect God to show up. *Hope* implies little certainty but suggests confidence or assurance in the possibility that what one desires or longs for will happen. This is the "what if there is a God" who might actually hear my prayers for something I need to happen. And the word *look* implies assurance that "expectations will be," that everything will work out. The *expect*ation that we have that our God will walk with us through the worst of the worst is where we *look* for Him, knowing that He's there. We *expect* to find Him in the darkness and when we do, that is the moment that *hope* comes alive. He gives us confidence and assurance that we are not alone and through Him all things are possible.

I find peace in that, in this one word. It is such a small word that brings such a big impact of whether we sit down in our valley moments or we stand up. It's praising in the midst of tragedy instead of crying and fighting for happiness instead of falling into fear. I expect God to be present in all my woes and I trust him whole heartedly. Many years back I wouldn't have been able to say that. But I say it with much assurance today. Sure I believed back then, but only surface deep. And as I continue reading in Jeremiah 29:12-14, it reads, "***12*** *'Then you will call on me and come and pray to me, and I will listen to you.* ***13*** *You will seek me and find me when you seek me with all your heart.* ***14*** *I will be found by you,' declares the LORD, 'and will bring you back from captivity. I will gather you from all the nations and places where I have banished you,' declare the LORD, 'and will bring you back to the place from which I carried you into exile.'*"

How appropriate this is in where I called on Him, I sought Him out and He brought me to a safe place. So to back it up; let me take you on a journey where I was the main character, when hope came alive for me.

CHAPTER 5

H is for healing.

The year 1996 was when I realized that I needed God and I needed hope. Until that point, all was good with an "I got this" attitude. I believed that there was a higher being, never questioning his existence but never dwelling in the Word, much less having relationship. I went to church and served, but would I say I was in right with God, absolutely not. I thought being a Christian meant saying my prayers each night but the rest of the time, I had it, I would take care of whatever came my way. No worries, just closing down my day with the same prayer I've said since I was a little girl. No conversation, no discussion about the day, just, "now I lay me down to sleep..." It wasn't until my life came to a screeching halt with a phone call in the middle of the night that this changed.

The caller told me my husband was having an affair. Stop. Everyone please take a seat; I know I had to. First, this is a hard one to swallow in sharing this moment in my life, in our lives, with you. This is the space that I wish didn't exist and wish it was just a bad dream. This is where all is silent and all you hear is the nothing. To admit that our marriage has a flaw—a pretty big one at that—is to say that God can do just about anything with a mess. And it was a mess, but one worth dealing with.

In reading about betrayal in the Bible, the one person who understood about this subject best is Jesus. He experienced betrayal to the fullest on the first day of the Festival of Unleavened Bread. In Matthew 26:17, Jesus was there with the disciples enjoying the meal. Judas had already planned on giving up Jesus to the chief priests and was just waiting for the best opportunity. Jesus knew this but played along in this predicament. As Jesus was reclining with his twelve disciples, he said to them, "Truly I tell you, one of you will betray me." Now if I was Judas, I would be anxious about this comment, as were the others. No one wanted Jesus to think it was them and even Judas replied, "Surely you don't mean me, Lord?" He was playing it off pretty good, acting just as shocked as everyone else. But Jesus was sure to say in verse 23, "The one who has dipped his hand into the bowl with me will betray me." This was one of the best call-outs noted in history, in my opinion. So who do you think was sitting to his left? Judas was sitting to the left of Christ and had shared his bowl. Jesus knew ahead of time that Judas was going to betray him; he placed him to the left, which was a seat of honor. Even with the coming events, Jesus still demonstrated love towards Judas, giving us a lesson on true love and devotion to even those who have sinned against us. But this was not what I was thinking about with the phone in hand.

I hung up the phone and just sat there—stock still, as if I moved, I might lose it. If I moved, I might just believe it. If I moved, I might just move into another chapter in my life that had just become a very dark place. I sat there for what seemed an eternity holding my breath. Across the hall was my son, three-years-old, and in that moment all I wanted to do was run, jump in my car and find my husband. Find him with *her*. But I couldn't, I had responsibilities and so I had to wait. There were no cell phones back then (imagine that!), so I just had to wait. The ringing in my ears was deafening and all I could think about was leaving.

So I began to pack a bag. Packing everything that one would need with toiletries, clothing and a few personal items. I packed socks and shoes and was careful not to forget anything. As I carried it downstairs, I opened the door and calmly sat it in the middle of the driveway. It wasn't my bag I packed; it was his. As I locked the door and turned out the light; it was the most deafening sound that a light switch could make. It wasn't the light I turned out; it was my marriage, my forever happy ending story. The life I knew, the man I knew, had all somehow changed in that very moment. I knew I would never be the same in my heart and I knew that the meaning of marital love would also never be the same for me. I knew that I couldn't do it and knowing this was one of the most difficult decisions I would make for our family. This was the ultimate betrayal that I thought

I would never get over. How could I, how could I ever look at him in the same way? I also knew the time would come when he did return and so I thought about what I would say. It was then that I would give him the opportunity to tell the truth. What if the phone call was a prank? What if it was all just a misunderstanding? I wondered if I could turn the channel, or even better, pause the channel and try to figure out another plan. Then everything would be okay, right? I wanted a different channel where the husband and wife live happily ever after, blah, blah, blah. This was not my life, my situation, or my devastation. But, this was it, that was the one that I was given that day, and so I waited.

When the moment came, the small knock on the door, I walked slowly down the hall. The walk was difficult, and it felt as if I had mud in my shoes and the heaviness was clear as I leaned into the door. I quietly asked through the door this simple question, "Who were you with tonight?" The slight pause and the answers given were incorrect and in that very instant, time stood still. I leaned on the door, feeling so alone and never realized in that moment that my God, my Father was leaning there with me also, wiping my tears. I walked away from the locked door of my life defeated and walked upstairs and went to bed. Never giving a thought where he was going or what this would mean for our family. I just knew in this moment, the little boy across the hall was counting on me to make the right decision for our little family. And I knew then that I needed this God, the one that performs miracles and who could deliver to me hope, this small little word, in my darkest hour.

[*God is the only one who can deliver hope.*]

Questions for Your Journey

- Is there a time when you needed to heal from a situation given and you found refuge with God?

- Write down the moment you knew you were not alone.

CHAPTER 6

O is for optimism.

Over the next months, we sought counseling, hoping to find a reason to stay married. The only thing I could come up with was my son. And so he became the glue to this broken puzzle. He became the one thing that I held on to, to make what I was going through worth it. This is not how I envisioned life. I had to swallow my pride in this moment and do everything I could before I called it final. We continued counseling, but it wasn't working. The clinical focuses on our past and childhood issues were not what we needed from those sessions. What we needed was an anchor. I knew if we continued on this course we would for sure end this marriage and I would forever be an angry woman afraid to love, trust and forgive. So we got counseling from our pastor at the church we attended. In this counseling we invited God into our marriage, into our mess and took on God's view of marriage. In Ephesians 4:2-3 it reads, "Be completely humble and gentle; be patient, bearing with one another in love. Make every effort to keep the unity of the Spirit through the bond of peace." This is where I began to learn about hope. So we began, sometimes alone and sometimes together, but we were building back the pieces and seeing some resemblance of why we married. This was difficult, and I wanted to run, as fast and far away as possible. I

> *Inviting God into your marriage is like an anchor that holds you steady in the rough waters.*

wanted to do anything to make this feeling of unworthiness end. But I couldn't, not yet. I had someone else that I had to factor into this situation and contemplate how this would affect my son's life. All I could think of was my past childhood of two separate homes, with the pickups and drop offs and weekend visits. Although sometimes ending a marriage is what's best, in our situation, that we BOTH were willing to try was a key factor to making it work. It was the worst of battles, but ones worth fighting for—for me and my son. We continued the fight but, little did I know, the stress was affecting me. This is where life immediately took a turn for me, where my faith was unsteady and God now had my full attention.

Questions for Your Journey

- Describe a time where God had your full attention.

- Did you sit with Him for counsel? Pray for Him to be present in asking for help in a certain situation.

CHAPTER 7

P is for perseverance.

It was just prior to the battle for my marriage that I had become sick—all the time. The doctors weren't sure and chalked it up to depression with the usual medications. Nausea was now my constant companion and everything I ate, drank, or even thought about made me sick. I found a new doctor that did every test imaginable and what he found was a severe case of acid reflux. The years of meds and anti-depressants, the doctors "not believing that I felt sick" turned into two years and over that time became so severe that I had stopped eating altogether. I had also become lactose intolerant since giving birth to my son, which explained why I felt sick every day. Over the course of the next year, I weighed less than 90 lbs. and had developed a fear of eating because I didn't want to feel sick. It was in the next several months when the days blended and I was so drugged up on meds (that the doctors said would make me feel better), I had almost attempted to take my life. That's right, I said it. It's shameful to even think I would do such a thing. God must have been horrified and disappointed all at the same time. It's a moment that I am not proud of and frankly, one I barely remember. Here I had a marriage falling apart, a now four-year-old that needed me and I was so sick that I just couldn't think of spending another day living in it. I was so malnourished and delirious that most days I didn't know what was going on, nor did I realize what I was contemplating. The only bright light that I had was my son. And it was my son who saved my life with the one simple word, "Mom." There is a connection for me in this one word. The same is true with Mary Magdalene when she was looking for Jesus at the tomb. In

John 20, Mary is looking for Jesus' body. The disciples had left and returned home but she couldn't leave without knowing where they had put him. Mary saw two angels sitting in the tomb and they asked her why she was weeping. She responded saying that she was looking for Jesus' body and wanted to know where they had put him. She then turned and saw a man, but didn't know it was Jesus. This man then asked her why she was weeping and she answered that she was so distraught because she didn't know where Jesus' body was. She was not ready for the finality of Jesus being gone, and it wasn't until Jesus spoke out, "Mary!" that she realized who he was.

Sometimes when we are so consumed by our own situations, we cannot see what is happening around us. The same held true for me in that one moment that could have changed everything.

Even as I'm writing this I am reminded of how God saved me that day by delivering a call out from the littlest person who brought perseverance like a sucker punch with one word, my name known to my son; Mom. It's like people you meet by coincidence or a song on the radio that made you pull over in that "it was just what you needed to hear" kind of moment. He used my son to snap me out of the darkness, the same as Mary. He called out to me in order to get my attention from my delirious state and from downstairs the sweetest little voice called out "Mom;" my life took a turn. It was his little voice that brought me back to reality. I was horrified, me with a 9mm Beretta pointed at my head. What in the world was I thinking? I guess I wasn't, and that's when I knew I was lost, sick, and didn't know how to get back. The walls were too high, and the pit was so cold and I knew that I had officially entered a very dark place and I began looking for my return ticket. But what was I in such a hurry to get back to; a failed marriage, a failed body, and most of all, a failed spirit. I knew that where I was that God couldn't, much less, wouldn't want to find me. I was unreachable and unstoppable in my downward spiral. In the days following, my body began to shut down. My doctor hospitalized me hoping to save my life, trying to figure out what was wrong with me. Days went by with me unaware of life around me. Feeding tubes were the only thing I could remember in hopes to nourish my body. The only moment I remember is waking up in a small room with a bed, desk, chair and camera that was pointed at me. What in the world was happening and who was watching me? Have I lost my mind? Where has my husband put me? Where were my things? Where was my son? And where was God?

Looking back now, I know I wasn't alone in that room. Satan not only had a front-row seat, but he was hot on my trail. His smile, or rather smirk, must have been from ear to ear in this silent victory of jeopardizing my happiness, my life and my faith. He had almost won, almost succeeded in me taking my life, leaving my son without a mother. But at the moment all I was thinking was "where was God?" Too ashamed to admit that I had failed, wasting my life that was given was all I could think about. How do you get from here to there and where do you go from what seemed a bottomless pit to the top?

I'm sure about now you are all thinking of a time in your life when you've reached a place where you felt as if there was no turning back. Where rock bottom was slammed against your face so hard and all you can think of is the failure you've become. Or maybe you think the road back is so much farther in reaching your destination so you just give up and take the shortest route; the quick fix, while maintaining the status quo. Walking around in a zombie state going through the motions with whatever life brings your way. Or maybe, just maybe you could get ticked off like I did and say "not today!" This was me. I didn't ask for this. This was not the way I was going down. If I was going down, I was going down swinging!

As days turn into weeks, they told me I had major depression with an eating disorder. What?! Are you kidding me?! But as I looked in the mirror for the very first time and saw the image that was now my reflection, I realized it was someone I didn't even recognize. I had no idea who that girl was, so broken and lifeless. I had become a faithless shell of someone I once knew. Someone who would have always been so fierce about doing the right thing, standing up for herself, loving and believing in herself that I was ashamed to stand in front of her, this stranger in front of me I now had become. I let her down, I let my son down, but most of all I let God down.

So now looking at this reflection, it sounded about right given everything that led up to the point; I began to panic. So, doing what we all would do, I started making deals... with God. If you get me out of here; if you heal me; if you show up, I'll show up. Looking back, I see how my love and most of all, my faith was circumstantial with God. I weighed it only on the response on what He would do *FOR* me. How could I be so ignorant in understanding the relationship that only He wanted with me, with you, with us? There is no wheeling and dealing, there is just the trust of love.

Questions for Your Journey

- Write down a moment where God called out to you and changed the course of your life.

- What does perseverance mean to you? Describe a time in your life where you persevered when you didn't think you had it in you.

I learned a lot about myself in this place, as horrific as it was. They kept me in a room at the end of the hall with a locked door; so let's just say, He now had my full attention. What I found over the weeks was that I did not differ from those around me. We all had something, some tool of dealing with our own situations. Whether it is drugs, alcohol or self-hurt, we based it on circumstances in our lives, in our DNA and in our minds.

[*God is in the room.*]

After leaving, I would spend my days at the facility learning about myself, learning how to live with my new food allergies. I attended weekly meetings to gain comfort and support to get through the days. I got to a place where I had recovered and had healed from that experience. I would then visit with the group from time to time to just speak with ones that stood where I had stood, walking the same path hoping to help them through it; each one, teach one. Not wasting a save. This save was given but it was in my perseverance of believing in the word *hope* that He allowed for healing in my body, mind and marriage. It's in the never giving up where you leap forward and to never quit is the ability to achieve the unimaginable. More than not, when things are hard the outcomes are worth it, maybe even outstanding. Persevering through the challenge builds character, builds stamina, but most of all gives you hope for things to come.

CHAPTER 8

E is for endurance.

This now brings me to the word endurance. Endurance means to have the power to go through something unpleasant or hard and not give up. It's gritting your teeth, clenching your fists and fighting with all your might to get through those valleys and reach the other side. It's pulling out the stones and using them for good and believing that there is so much more than this… this moment.

As I write this, I think back on the memories that come flooding back. Our marriage was rescued, we now have three sons and we celebrated our 28th wedding anniversary this year! This was difficult… please know this. This was years in the making. But most good situations are preceded by a time when you must endure the unthinkable. Time is a precious thing and God's view on time is very specific. He reminds us in the Scriptures that there will be many things that will distract us. Psalm 31:15 reads, "My times are in your hands; Deliver me from the hands of my enemies, from those who pursue me." This one speaks volumes about the enemy always being nearby, filling our day with useless activities or habits that create feelings of anxiety when we stand still. How many times are we too busy to give time to family, friends or God in the midst of our busyness? Remember, I was almost too busy to take part in that bible study. But time is what we need to reflect, adjust and move forward.

So that is what we did in our marriage. In Proverbs 16:9, "In their hearts humans plan their course, but the Lord establishes their steps." You always hear that time heals all wounds and I believe that wounds can heal where there is God. It wasn't until we invited God into our marriage, into our lives, that we began to heal. We learned about love, true love and what it means to love. In Matthew 11:28 it reads, "Come to me, all you who are weary and burdened, and I will give you rest." We were tired. We were fragile, but within those moments, He gave us rest. He gave us hope, and He gave us love again. He taught us what true love is, in those moments of doubt. To remember that love is kind, patient, and giving is where we found Him amidst our mess. He gives hope when we need it and even when we don't deserve it. He gave me my fierceness back to know who I am and believe that through all of this there was and is hope. These four simple letters that spell a word with so much punch, with so much meaning that changed my life.

> *When life gets hard, stand up when you want to sit down.*

In this word there is H: healing, O: opportunity, P: perseverance, and E: endurance. God showed me hope in the worst time of my life. It didn't happen overnight, and it didn't happen easily. I took it in the chin and I stood up when I wanted to sit down. It took every ounce of determination to survive for this one little boy, my sweet boy, who called out my name and God reminded me who I am: a child of God.

Questions for Your Journey

- Describe a time where HOPE came alive for you.

H for Healing:

O for Opportunity:

P for Perseverance:

E for Endurance:

Raw Faith

"Now, O Jacob, listen to the LORD who created you. O Israel, the one who formed you says, "Do not be afraid, for I have ransomed you. I have called you by name; you are mine. When you go through deep waters, I will be with you. When you go through rivers of difficulty, you will not drown. When you walk through the fire of oppression, you will not be burned up; the flames will not consume you."

~ Isaiah 43:1-2

CHAPTER 9

What if life is not about you?

That sentence is challenging. I had to sit here and think about that sentence and what it means to me. So what if it's not? Just as in parenting you learn about patience and the act of being selfless in where being a parent takes priority. We define the true definition of selfless as, "concerned more with the needs and wishes of others than with one's own; unselfish or an act of selfless devotion".

I know I can remember back as my children were born my needs and wants became further and further from the top of my "To Do" list. The hair appointments were non-existent, the workouts became squats at the changing table and the shopping trips all became short frenzy bursts between feeding times. It was a good day if you didn't have spit up in your hair and a ponytail was now your new look. But that's what you do, you sacrifice. If this is where you're at, just hear me when I say "it's temporary" and I love you. All of us mothers understand and stand beside you on this battlefield. I know how tired you are, exhausted even, but just remember that these small little humans are blessings, so believe that even in the moments you don't.

I'm now in a season of motherhood where I have two who are married and one still in high school. Having raised my boys with an open door policy through faith, there was many times I had to stand on their path; between them and the enemy. If you hear anything from me about teenage years, hear this; do not step off the path. Continue to be engaged and available. And be that tiger momma when the moments arise. Meaning, there are moments that circumstances need to be lessons. But sometimes there are lessons that need your attention. But in no way do you ever quit fighting for their spirit and heart. This I would have to say is one of the most critical times for parents to be present in their children's lives. And this brings me to a yearlong battle for my son in where I found him on a detour.

This is a hard place to be as a teenager. Let's just say it was a difficult year of a season for him with new beginnings. But for my son, it was more of him trying to find himself while everything in his life was changing. He is a lot like me in that we like to be in control of every situation all the time. And this detour he found himself on was a dark place. The moment I want to talk about is the moment that I flung the door open and stood in the face of fear and I fought for my son.

I remember the moments of doubt where I was not sure if I could reach him. This was months of rebellion and the spreading of his wings, and I prayed over and over again to just be able to speak words over him that he needed to hear. When the time came with the surge of emotion that overwhelmed me, I flung open his door and said, "Not today!" As he spun around in his chair, the look of being so lost was so evident to me. I recognized that look, that same face that I had worn in my past. As moms, we protect; that's what we do from the very moment we find out they even exist. We are the first to know them, to feel their movement and we are always there, no matter what. And over the course of their lives, we stand on their path; in guiding their steps, teaching right from wrong, growing them into strong, happy humans. So when we see them hurting, it hurts us. They are a piece of us; an extension out in this world.

So, now standing in front of my son, I don't back down; from the enemy. As I began to speak that day, I spoke love over him whether he wanted to hear it or not. I told him that I know of this dark place, this cold bottomless pit; the one his face is pressed against and that I would never give up or leave him there. I told him I believed in him and I would sit there with him until he was ready. I knew this place; I was familiar with this place. As the tears welled in his eyes, I began to see my son for the first time in a very long time. As we began to talk about the "just looking up" part, that God is just waiting to be noticed and acknowledged in his darkness, is where I began to see the light on his face.

I continued speaking about the never being alone; even at the bottom. We talked for a while, it was the most time I had spent with him in a long time. We talked about life and the next season for him and talked about what was important to him and the dreams he had. I told him I saw such great potential for his future even when he could not. Sometimes you get off the path and take detours; and that's okay; and he needed to hear that. But with me lending a save to my son that day, in sharing an ugly, that helped change his course. We began to see him grow stronger in his faith and today, he is a changed man. I've never been so proud of him for facing the opposition head on. Do not ever step off their path. God never steps off ours and He allows the detours for growth and gives us free will.

MOM = Managing Opportunities Masterfully.

Although I miss those times with those little faces looking at me for everything and the little hands holding mine, the season of teenagers can be challenging but also amazing. We moms and dads teach them to do for themselves, in being independent; just as God teaches us. And just as our little ones grow, we as parents still want to have a relationship with our children. And our God is just the same. Our God is a jealous God with a longing to be in relationship with each and every one of us daily. He stands on your path, so meet Him there. I just have to believe that I am not the only mom who has told their child that "it's not all about them". What if "it's not all about us"? What if what we want is not the plan? In finding and experiencing life in a new way, do we call that faith; or how about raw faith?

Questions for Your Journey

- What does raw faith mean to you?

- Can you recall a moment in time when someone stood on your path in love that changed your direction?

CHAPTER 10

How do you get raw faith?

I facilitated my first Bible study on raw faith and what I discovered was that to have that kind of faith, it takes surrender. Surrendering to whatever life deals you, pushing all your chips in and saying, "Let's do this… you lead and I will follow." So what does that look like on earth? What I found is that faith lies in the heart of believing in something bigger than you can imagine. So how do you get it? How does one find true faith? How do you find a raw faith that is unbridled and rejects the enemy at every turn by igniting our hearts to the very One who created us?

This leads me to a man whose faith was undeniable. His faith was so fierce that nothing could shake him. I talk about this man several times because his faith was unshakable. His name was Job, and he was very intentional about avoiding sin. He lived with his family and was blessed with great wealth. God was so pleased with him he boasted about this to an angel named "Satan." Satan told God that Job was only this way because of what God had given him and asked if he could test him by sending trials his way. God agreed, having great confidence that Job would stay true in his faith.

It is through a course of four trials and being stripped of everything that Job was tested. They all were horrible, much more than most could comprehend. They were great losses including all of his flocks, his servants and his ten children. The final trial was a skin disease that covered his body. But Job not once ever scorns God for his situation, only praises Him through it. It is in our great suffering that we find the depths of our sorrow, but it is also in those depths where we find ourselves, our strength in the Lord, and our raw faith.

Sound easy? How do you wrap your mind around those moments of faith where the circumstances of life do not determine our level of faith? The act of giving it all up, to lift the first and very best to our Lord, even in the trenches; in understanding and finding peace that whatever decision that is given to you is in your best interest. To have this faith is an all-consuming and easier situation if we just submit to His will for our lives. But we like to muddy it up, create drama, and find dissatisfaction in the "no's" that come our way. To have the true faith from within is not to doubt in the plans He has for each of us, but to believe that our purpose is for His benefit only. What if this life is not about me or you? What if you are part of the bigger plan? The reason you came to be, the reason you have those incredible gifts and talents; what if they were for His purpose only?

So how do you get it; true and fierce faith? How do you go all in? Every day I strive to achieve the fiercest faith I can get. Sometimes I make it out the door and stumble, tripping out the door, but believe me; I fight to get up… every day. To believe that it's okay even when things get hard or even painful, that the true test of faith believes that no matter what, God's got this. That's my goal each day; to trust that He has us from the very beginning to the very end.

John the Baptist, who devoted his entire life to following God and died doing what God had planned for him, never wavered in his faith. And God was pleased. God was pleased, people! John exhibited true faith in giving all that he had to what was good, true, and just. And God was pleased. Jesus said in Matthew 10:39, "Whoever finds their life will lose it, and whoever loses their life for my sake will find it." What does that mean? John died by calling out King Herod on his sinful ways and was beheaded. End of chapter, right? Maybe for John's life here on earth but the heavenly treasures are so much more than we could ever imagine. John's devotion to doing and living out God's purpose and displaying obedience is a testimony of what true faith looks like.

[*God was pleased!*]

In the chapters of my life, with the decisions I've made and the constant control that consumes me, He still saves me every day. It is through those saves where His most outstanding work is done. In those valley moments He sifts and refines us in the building of our faith.

I once heard and find comfort in knowing that there are two paths to every decision that we make. I guess that gives us a 50/50 shot to make the right decision. With each decision comes a consequence, which lays the groundwork of the next decision and determines how the path continues to branch out. The hope is we make the right decisions which will lead us to whatever He has planned. I'm sure my life looks like a complicated road map with many twists and turns. He allows these detours called our own will, or rather free will, those decisions that were sometimes not the best. But within the next decision we choose the path less traveled; winding us back on track.

Questions for Your Journey

- List your gifts and talents; what do you love and what comes easily to you?

- Recall a detour you have taken that led you astray. Have you gotten back on the path? If not, write a prayer asking God for the direction in which to go.

A path less traveled is living a life for Christ and like Christ. A life of discipline in a materialistic world where the constant attractiveness of sin is around every corner is daunting. The path is narrow, but knowing and recognizing the difference between gifts and godly gifts is where our lives come alive.

Matthew 7:14 reads, "But small is the gate and narrow the road that leads to life and only a few find it."

A few… what?! I highlight this text because I remember the first time I read this. I sat there with my mouth open and decided right then it was my goal to be one of the few. I don't have it all together, but every day this one verse gives me a reason to try.

So how does this relate to me in my not-so-good choices and decisions? Well, let's just say that I used to be so in control of my life, in every decision, that there wasn't room for anything or anyone else. I was so quick to make things happen that I ran from just about anything that would require me to feel anything. But, boy was I good at organizing everyone else's lives, ministries, or feel good causes that kept me from ever having to engage with anyone on a personal level.

There are women out there who can relate, I'm sure. Who of you are the good organizers, the team moms, the room moms, the ones who create opportunities for others to participate in, so that you can avoid real communication or relationships? Raise your hand if you're the busy one. My hand is raised! But the moment someone says, "Let's do lunch," you freeze, fearful you'll be committing to a relationship. So you think, just talk to the hand, keep them busy, or at least appear to be busy and all the while things are getting done, for everyone else. What does Scripture say about living in community?

There are many Scriptures on community in living together and loving each other. My favorite of these is Matthew 18:20, which reads, "For where two or three gather in my name, there am I with them." Community means to live amongst others and to live in fellowship with others by sharing life together. It's about sharing successes, struggles, and all the in between moments within a group and lifting each other up. Although I know this, I still seem to keep my distance and never fully engage.

So why do we become so disengaged and too unwilling to share our lives? Why do we covet loneliness and lonely places? Why are we afraid to reveal our emotions with others? What if they find out I don't have it all together?

But this is where Satan sets the stage and becomes the director of your life. So what if they think you're a hot mess and they find out you may feed your kids Lucky Charms for dinner on Friday "pantry night?" Pantry night is when it's been a long week; you give yourself the night off, and open up the pantry, making dinner from whatever's inside.

What if they find out you are so out of touch with your feelings you create tasks in your life so you don't have time to feel them? What if they say that you're a terrible mother? "Look at you, why would your husband find you beautiful? Your hair is a mess, your house is not perfect, you're putting on the pounds and have you done the yard work yet? Goodness girl, get it together!" These are things I would hear in my head; keeping me alone in my solo status in making others think I'm too busy for friendships. Satan loves to sit in the corner when you're alone and spout out these lies, telling you that you do not have time for friendships, time to invest in family, no time for Bible studies, and no time for God.

Believe you can
And you will!

So here are my thoughts, for what it's worth. God knows I need a new day, each day to get it right. I think we all need that. How many times have you just had a bad day? The alarm clock doesn't go off, your kids aren't cooperating in getting ready fast enough, and you've now become the mom who's nagging them to move faster. There's traffic, you're late for work, they're late for school and it doesn't matter how hard you try, nothing is going right. When you get home, you just want to go to bed and start over. You feel as if you've failed and you'll just have to try again tomorrow. But here is the good news. The next day, tomorrow, is a new day. Yesterday already happened and today I will get it right. Step out of the loneliness and find peace in getting real with others. When you *out* the enemy and his lies and find people to stand by your side, you can and will be unstoppable. *That is living in community.*

Questions for Your Journey

- List at least two people that you can trust and pursue to be in community with.

- How can you reach out today and include them in your life? (e.g. dinner, coffee, shopping, beach time)

I have this plaque in two areas of my house, "Believe You Can and You Will." It's mind over matter, right? But sometimes my faith was lacking on this topic. When things go wrong for a long stretch of time, your faith gets bruised along the way. I can remember a season where it was all I could do not to doubt my faith, but God had another thought. What if He stripped me down and started over? Hitting bottom is necessary to reset priorities, where the noise is so deafening in our lives we lose sight of His presence. So this was the end of the past and the beginning of my new life. Little did I know that my life was about to change and it would not be pretty.

CHAPTER 11

The surrendering begins.

The year was now 2008, when everything I believed in changed in an instant. We were eleven years beyond the "learning about hope days" and three kids later. Sometimes change is necessary in a reset moment, but for us, we were about to experience a re-do. Not "that hurt a little" change but the kind that brings you to your knees. It was within this year of being humbled that I found God standing on the path waiting for me to notice His existence again. Or rather, He stormed into my life, shook it down, stripped me bare and took a seat in my heart. I realized then that He stood beside me all those years, but I was once again too busy to notice. Still. Ugh. The blame game had once again become my coping mechanism and I was looking to blame someone fast. Sure, I acknowledged His presence, but I still had that "I can do all things through me" attitude, which still wasn't working. The patience of our God is remarkable and from my very first breath to forty years later must have been torture for Him. It's like watching water boil. Watching me handle it, taking control... I can do it on my own was my motto and must have been painful to watch. But it wasn't until I surrendered my life in this moment and came to the end of me and my plans that He took a place in my heart and called it home; I knew I would never be the same.

It all started in my car listening to KLOVE. I had found the station by accident... Okay, if you want to believe that "weird kind of moment" was accidental. Anyway, a song about praising Him in the storm had come on. As I listened to the song I thought, "How could I praise anyone, much less God, in our situation?"

My husband had been laid off. My job had taken a turn for the worst, meaning I was commission only and the real estate market sank. We had three small boys living in a home that we now could not afford. We had very little funds to pay the necessities, much less the credit that we had racked up, not to mention no health insurance. Everything that we had worked for was gone; everything was drained—bank accounts, savings accounts and my faith, and our faith as a family. Every part of me was being affected.

As I listened to the lyrics I thought, praising in this situation would be very difficult for me. I always like to feel in control of the situation and I've lived up to my expectations of *what I thought* was being a good person. How could He do this to me, as if being a good person was enough? How could He do this to us, my family, and my boys? But as I sang that song, I realized in that moment that loving God had nothing to do with my paycheck or bank account. It had nothing to do with my situation. It had nothing to do with my materialistic losses. That night I loved Him anyway and I sang my heart out. I say I have the rug burns on my nose from the humbling experience that I was in, but looking back it was just what I needed. He had to strip me bare of all distractions, saying "Hey, remember Me, I'm over here."

This moment in life reminds me once again of Job. He was a man blessed by God, but Satan declared that the only reason Job loved God was because God protected and blessed him. So to prove Satan wrong, God gives him permission to take all of Job's wealth, health, and children. His three friends counsel him and debate God's intentions, but Job stays true in his faith, not demanding an explanation. He stays ***silent*** in front of the Lord and God blesses him even more than before.

Questions for Your Journey

❖ Recall a time where you also had the rug burns on your nose to gain your attention.

❖ Is there a time in your life when things or people were taken away and you didn't know why? How did you respond in this situation?

Sometimes during life we became so engrossed in our to-do's, desires and need for approval that we forget that God is even in the room. The very thought of that, that He is in the room, in our lives, every day is crazy to think about. This is the creator of the universe people, and I was blaming him! What I learned was my to-do's were all-consuming, my wants were unnecessary and the only approval that I needed was from the One person I ignored. Don't get me wrong, I went to church. Check that box. I sang in church, check that box too. But did I worship? You think tapping my foot and thinking about my grocery list while singing in church is honoring or what we call worshiping? The definition of the Greek word worship" is "to bow down" or "to fall down before." In no way is my tapping foot falling down. I guess what I'm saying is that when you are right with God and the Holy Spirit lives within you, the Holy Spirit sings out to the Lord. This is the Lord we are talking about. Never give Him second best!

Praise Him in your storm. Praise Him FOR your storm.

So back to the song on KLOVE, and me feeling not so happy about the situation I was in; I began to sing this song... out loud. The sobs that were exploding from me were extraordinary and uncontrollable; I had to stop the car. Whatever happened in that moment was life-changing. I praised Him *for* my mess. I praised Him *for* my children. I praised Him *for* my marriage. I praised Him *for* being who He is. I praised Him *in* my storm. I praised Him *FOR* my storm.

Looking back, I see where He attempted to gain my attention. But it was in the defining moment of stripping me down to having nothing that I looked up. It was in that moment of praising Him when I had nothing to give that He shook me to my very core. It was where I placed my eyes upon Him for the first time in a long time. He sat down, pulled up a chair, and became the sole provider of my life that very day. It was like I had come home from a very long detour and I was back on the path.

Questions for Your Journey

- Think about a time when you surrendered a situation and God showed up big. Be detailed in giving Him a hallelujah!

CHAPTER 12

How deep is your faith?

So how deep is your faith? Is it bone deep or is it muscle deep? Bone deep is the faith that no matter what you are facing, you find comfort that God is in control. Nothing can shake you and you praise Him through it. Muscle deep is somewhere in the middle, that when things are okay, you're good. Your faith is solid and business as usual. But when things don't go as planned or there's disappointment, you question His intentions and so then you question your faith. I have a full understanding of this faith. I question His intentions all the time and always conclude that they are good. But it still doesn't make it easy. It is in the valleys that your faith has potential to grow—explode even! There are things learned within those detours of life that trigger some discussions with the one and only God. My take on these discussions is that He is my Father and with that sometimes comes a conflict of interest. I mean that in the highest respect, but my position is that He appreciates my input, or so I think. It doesn't mean that He will change His mind, but the mere thought that I can come to Him for counsel confirms that my love and recognition of his approval is important; worthy as a father is to a child.

How many times when you were a child did you throw a fit when you didn't what you wanted... sometimes even on the floor? Your parent would watch you, talk with you about whatever the issue was, but if it was not in your best interest, the answer would still be "no." The same is true in our relationship with God. He is our Father who wants nothing but good for us. He looks out for us and decides the yes and no answers. As a child we succumbed to the fact that our parent was, most of the time, correct in this guidance, and so should we be okay with His. Although it may feel in your darkest moment, it's not. In the depths of despair there is darkness, true. But it is in that darkness where only God's light will guide us through this thing called life.

I realized in analyzing my faith I measured it by what my experience was in that moment. What experience am I going through right now? If it's good, then hallelujah! Just like the Israelites. If it's just okay, not getting the answer I'm looking for, hallelujah anyway! If it's an event that is gut-wrenching, life-changing or just plain horrible, then hallelujah! How hard is it to say that and believe it? You just have to do it, say it like you mean it. Even if you don't believe it in the beginning, somewhere in the middle you see His hand in all that you do. It is in this doing, *on purpose*, intentional act of showing true faith, that His whispers become vibrant and alive.

Faith is the understanding and belief that Jesus died on a cross for our sins. It should have nothing to do with your circumstance or not getting the answers you want. It is in the just saying "Halleluiah, praise God anyway!" Praising Him in the storms... praising Him in the moments of joy, praising Him on the mountaintop highs but most of all, praising Him through the valley lows where He never leaves our side, is true faith. He is the rock at the bottom, the one your face is pressed against or slammed into. It is letting our faith stand strong during every moment of our lives and that, my friend, is showing true faith, bone deep; the good stuff. Believing and being okay with His timing, with His answers and loving Him through it, no matter what, is true, raw, and fierce faith.

Questions for Your Journey

- ❖ What is one thing you can do to add community into your life? (Ex: join a Bible study, call a friend, volunteer, etc.)

- ❖ Recall a time in your life where you were humbled. What did you do with it?

Perseverance

"Let us not become weary in doing good, for at the proper time we will reap the harvest if we do not give up."
~ Galatians 6:9

CHAPTER 13

Run like you mean it.

There's a friend called perseverance or rather what I call discipline. I revisited this word while training for a marathon. Yep, that's right; I did that. I love running. I admire the ones who run multiple marathons and can't wait for the next. I admire the ones who break records and strive to beat their best times, but I just love to run. Short bursts, sometimes longer ones, but anything over 15 miles is just plain nuts!

So what is perseverance? The official definition is "steadfastness in doing something despite difficulty or delay in achieving success." And that is what I did or had through this experience of grace.

I bet you didn't know that God has a training program. A training program is not for the weary but for one who can go the distance. Just as in marathon training, they don't give us the whole sixteen weeks of training schedules in advance. Believe me that would eliminate a lot of runners on day one. They gave us our run schedules every month so we would not be overwhelmed by seeing the increase in miles of training. Can you imagine if God gave you your life in a book and you could look ahead but not able to change a thing?

A biblical parallel to the marathon is the story of David, yet again. We read earlier how he went into the battle with his five smooth stones and conquered the giant, Goliath. After defeating the Philistine, King Saul was very fond of David, the teenage conquering hero. But over time he began to feel threatened by David's popularity. So he devised a plan to have him killed. David escaped into the desert and there he stayed for ten years relying only on the Lord and being trained by Him. *In Psalm 59:16-17, he says of God, "But I will sing of your strength, in the morning I will sing of your love; for you are my fortress, my refuge in times of trouble. You are my strength, I sing praise to you; you, God, are my fortress, my God on whom I can rely."*

It was after Saul's death that God chose David to become King of Israel and he reigned for forty years. In the beginning they had overlooked him but with God's training and having an open heart in trusting Him, God prepared him and God will prepare you for future successes.

Questions for Your Journey

❖ Describe a time that felt like a training moment where God was training you for your future.

❖ What did you learn about yourself?

❖ What were the steps that He required of you in order to grow to the next level?

David met God in the desert. I met Him on mile 22 of a marathon in 2016. I had turned 50 that year and I not only did this crazy thing, but I also graduated from college. That's another chapter on perseverance up ahead. But to tell you how I became steadfast in doing this run, let me start from the beginning of my running career.

It begins when you get this bright idea to do something that seems impossible and you become fixated, almost obsessed, until you've completed that task. Or at least that's me in a nutshell on most things. Some call it OCD, I call it being tenacious. So six years prior to this marathon I couldn't run to my mailbox. I was twenty pounds fluffier, we were in the "praise you in the storm" days and the stress was unbearable. I had heard that running was a stress reliever and I had a friend who ran who always looked stress-free, so I announced that I would go run. My husband looked at me and stated that I don't run. Knowing this, I acknowledged and agreed with him, but I declared that today I now would run. I got the shoes, I got the shorts, my ear buds and I walked out to the road. I had never given a thought to *how* I should run. I just thought you did it—*that,* my friend, was the first of many mistakes when learning the skill of running.

There is a lot that is happening all at the same time and to get in sync while listening to a song is an art. Not to mention the dodging of cars and animals. But I put on my playlist and started to run. I ran to the first mailbox, and I had a take a break; I am serious. So I walked to the next mailbox. Once there, I ran to the next mailbox and then time for the next break. So a pattern was forming, and I began running every other mailbox. The road I live on is long, and I found that I could run/walk for quite some time doing this strategy that I've now discovered. Little did I know that there is training like this called interval training, but like I said, I was new to this sport. This became quite exhilarating, and I found that over time I felt better, started eating better and started slimming down.

So as the months turned into years I began to run every two mailboxes, to every block, to the tree, to whatever landmark I set to stretch my distance. I then began to run miles and did that for years. I never reached any distance over four miles and always ran by myself. My friends had no interest, as they said in "torturing themselves" running somewhere when they could drive, so I continued to be solo in my running career.

But what I found that grew was my prayer time. By listening to my music; I was praising and worshiping all the way down the road. I've cried, sometimes to the point of having to stop and collect myself, because if you didn't know already, it's almost impossible to run while crying; you can but it's not pretty. Try it… it doesn't work. But I would run early in the morning and be in awe of his canvases in the sky. I found it was a time set aside for God where He had my attention and used that time for good. I found that during these runs over time something that formed was a "relationship." Isn't that what we all want, what God wants? I have to say that having a relationship with God has changed my life. No longer is He this big guy sitting up in the sky. He is my Father in Heaven who I go to for counsel, who I share my celebrations with, and the one who I go to for my difficult moments. He gives me peace in my heart and I believe in His word.

> *Having a relationship with God changes your life.*

In 2 Timothy 1:7 it reads, "For the Spirit God gave us does not make us timid, but gives us power, love and self-discipline." So while challenging myself, I found satisfaction in my small victories just going down the road. I would, at times, stop and look up in the quiet morning as if it was just He and I, and would wonder if He could see little 'ole me just standing in the road. And what I found is that He did.

CHAPTER 14

Angels in our midst.

I am sure that God has a way with each one of us of letting us know that He's there. You may feel a nudge, a sign, a small twinge that pulls at your heart and swivels your thoughts toward Him when you need Him. God has a sense of humor when calling me out and letting me know He's near.

An example of this is my fascination with blue herons. They are majestic and every time I see them I am in awe of their beauty. Their stature draws my attention every time. Toward the end of my college education, when I was in turmoil about my future, I found myself in tears most of the time while running. God displayed His presence four times through these amazing creatures. It became clear by the fourth time that He was just letting me know I was not alone in these decisions I was facing.

The first sighting was in my bathroom at home. Wait a minute that sounds weird; Let me explain. My bathroom is on the second level and I have two windows. The houses are close and I can see the top of my neighbors roofline just out the transom window. Opposite the window is a mirrored closet door, and I was doing my "face painting," as my children called it. My music was playing, I was singing and there he was. Touching down on my neighbor's roof, with a wing span that can reach between 5.5 to 6.5 feet and standing 3.2 to 4.5 feet tall, was what looked like a prehistoric creature—a great blue heron. With his long legs and graceful way he was staring at me in an awkwardly amazing moment. I didn't think much of it at the time; I was just amazed by its beauty as we stood there and just stared at each other.

A few days later, the second encounter was during a run. My thoughts began to go to God as I came across these birds. I had just turned up my main road and a woman was walking down her driveway to her mailbox. As she turned, I was passing her from the other side, and she bent down to pull a weed. It was in that very moment a heron came from behind me, buzzing me, and flew over the path of the road. I was so shocked at the size, having not ever been that close that I then realized that the lady never even saw him. She stood up and made her way to the house as if nothing happened. I had stopped in the road and just stood there, mouth open and felt overwhelmed by something I call being in the "stillness." You know the kind where everything around you just slows down and you recognize the quietness in the freeze frame moment. Sometimes in our lives where you just know and believe the moment has been created for just you. You can't explain it and it seems weird to those around you and they just nod as if to say you're crazy. But considering the stress I was under to make these big decisions when nothing was working out, I realized doubt about my path and fear was setting in. These moments God created just for me. He does that sometimes as if to say, "I'm still here."

Being in the presence of God is being in the stillness.

A few days later it was drizzling and I went out for a run. It had been an emotional day, and I needed clarity. As I neared my entrance I had stopped running, because of the coordination thing of crying and running. I saw something down the road standing in the middle of road. I started to run, but I slowed my pace and strained to make out what it was. And there it was, God dressed as a heron; just standing in the road. The silence was deafening. The rain was so quiet, as if it too also knew His presence was there. There were no cars, and he didn't seem startled by me. We just stood there staring at each other in the rain. I had to take a seat right there on the curb and praise Him in my storm, in this storm, that He would think enough of me to let me know that He saw me in the road.

How many times do those moments go unnoticed by each one of us? The moments where He attempts to let us know that He's right beside us throughout our day by giving us small nudges; where we dodge them all day long.

The final moment of his tapping on my shoulder was several weeks after when I was exiting my neighborhood on my bike. My decisions about school still had not panned out and I needed the assurance that I was still on the right path in the waiting, in the being still. I have a wall in the front of my neighborhood and so I'm not able to see the street until I exit. As I turned the corner on my bike, there he was—standing in the road! I am not kidding; as if to say, "Hello again." I could only smile and feel touched knowing that my God, my Father in Heaven was reaching out and reminding me that I needed to trust in His timing. He was saying, "Don't worry, just keep moving and persevere and I'll provide the way." There are those times in our lives that He just lets us know He's there. I used to miss it all the time. Those little moments, the hints of His presence that is so clear to an open heart. He's all around you so don't miss out on those "coincidental" moments. Or those moments where you scream "That was so crazy!" or "I don't know how that happened!" Yes you do; He is crazy in love with you and you know how that happened, and somewhere deep in your heart you know it's true.

Some may say that it's just a bird, and he lives in your neighborhood and is stalking you... Yes maybe. But, it is not coincidental that the exact moments I encountered that bird were the moments I most needed to hear from God and He knew that. And the instant I came in the presence of this amazing bird, the one worthy of "my stillness," my thoughts turned to God and He gave me peace. Immediately I felt overwhelmed and surrounded by His love. I know it was Him because my heart was open and now I cherish each of those moments.

In Romans 1:20, "For since the creation of the world God's invisible qualities, his eternal power and divine nature, have been clearly seen, being understood from what has been made, so that people are without excuses." If we believe in the Creator and accept everything began with His hands, then we'll be aware of those glorious moments in which He reveals himself all around us.

Questions for Your Journey

- List out moments, like my heron moments, that you knew it was God? Be aware of them and find peace.

CHAPTER 15

Running a marathon is facing a giant.

For all you runners, I know you will appreciate the will and determination that it takes to tackle the challenge of a marathon. It's a challenge of the mind, heart and soul and only those who have embarked on this path can understand. Sure, there are other things just as daunting, but there is something about your feet hitting the ground and going the distance that makes this human breed different. Did you know, as of today, that only 0.5% of the U.S. population have run a marathon? So this marathon thing was a giant for me.

For years I ran by myself and I did pretty much the same thing, same route year after year. I started to feel as if I needed a change in stepping out of my comfort zone. Sometimes in life we get stagnant and we wake up every morning and go to sleep at the same time and the days blend together. Stretching ourselves daily, where you push a little further, do something a little better or just challenge yourself to figure out what life is all about, is what I call living. So wanting this change, I signed up with a training group through a local running establishment where they set a running schedule and taught me to run long distance. I trained for a half marathon the year prior and did the unimaginable; I ran it. The training was difficult, the hours put in were numerous, and the sense of accomplishment of what I'd previously thought an impossible task was rewarding. It felt incredible to push myself out of my daily box and experienced self-worth, determination, and discipline differently. I was among people that were crazier than I was and I was satisfied, or so I thought.

Little did I know that six months later I would sign up for a full marathon! What was I thinking? I know what I was thinking... during my half marathon run, when all the full marathoners were veering off from our shared route to extend their run an extra 13.1 miles, I thought to myself that they were insane. I was crazy but thought there is no way I would ever do that... who in their right mind would run 26 miles—on purpose? Oh, wait... 26.2 miles. The .2 has a clearly defined meaning to us runners. The .2 is the most difficult part of the whole 26 miles. How could that be possible, right? Just like anything in life, you accomplish a task, no matter how hard or difficult, and just when you are at the finish line, you give up. Right there when you're so close in tackling the challenge that you've set out for yourself and almost conquered, you give up in the final steps. You complicate it by setting obstacles in your way, doubt in your mind that you might not complete it and say the word "can't," which is a bad word in my household, and you never finish.

> *The .2 is the hardest than the whole of a marathon.*

Saying the word "can't" is a sure fire way of not accomplishing anything. And you're right, you never will. Just like the word "impossible." To say that something is impossible is just another word for not trying. I think I've heard that in a song. Anyway, the .2 is the opt-out moment that we all look for when things get tough. If something is easy, it's not worth as much to finish, but if something takes time and only a few ever finish, then the outcome is pretty awesome. The road less traveled, so to speak. So by saying that something is hard, even impossible, you give yourself an excuse to quit. And that is the enemy of success, stirring up doubt.

Questions for Your Journey

- Think of a time that you used the word "impossible." Change it to *I'm Possible.*

- What if you did what you thought was impossible? How would that change your life?

Now the next turn of events in this training gave me a good reason to say "I can't" or "it's impossible." A month before I was to run the 26.2 mile beast, I became injured. I had been training for twelve weeks, run hundreds of miles, produced buckets of sweat and to be injured and possibly unable to complete the race was unacceptable. I did all the right things, rolled it out, iced it, and heated it; even cutting my runs down hoping to repair it. When my run coach told me it would not be healed by race day, it devastated me. Either I would have to skip it and wait for the next one or figure out how to do it injured.

Well, me being me; I was up for the challenge. Are you kidding me?! So I pressed on and a week and a half out I felt good, running long miles and *boom*. There it was again rearing its ugly head. The night before the run, all I could do was stay off of it and hope for the best. But I was limping, dragging my wooden leg across the floor because when an IT band goes out, it's ugly. It's where your knee stiffens up and does not bend, which is a necessary movement in the running, of course. It is almost impossible to walk much less run a marathon. You can't even pretend. How was I going to run?

Isn't this the way life goes? You prepare and plan for life's events, and then something always makes it impossible. How bad do you want it, right? My memory verse in this moment was from Galatians 6:9, "Let us not become weary in doing good, for at the proper time we will reap a harvest if we do not give up." A perfect example of a man who faced many trials and continued to persevere is the Apostle Paul. I often think of him when trying to keep perspective in my own situation. And although he faced many trials of being beaten, stoned, and faced death many times, he remained faithful and focused in serving God. I encourage you to read about the Apostle Paul to find encouragement when in a difficult spot.

So you push yourself to find other avenues, other ways of doing things, and this is where perseverance comes in—or we quit. That would be easy, but perseverance is hard. But we all have it inside of us, and it challenges us to ask ourselves just how bad do you want it?

> *Quitting would be easy.*

So I decided that I would show up early and tape up and just see what happened. I prayed for good legs; I prayed for endurance; I prayed for my Heavenly Father to be with me. The challenging part of this was that I could not run with my pace group I had just trained with the last sixteen weeks. This was my team, my encouragers, my running warriors. I was running by myself, my ear buds and my amazing husband meeting me at pre-planned spots on the course. That would be my next five something hours of what seemed impossible.

I showed up, took the mark and watched my group run ahead. My leg hurt from the very first step but I ran slow and steady. I prayed... the entire time. At the pre-marked spots, there was my husband. I would just burst out in tears just seeing him. My leg was holding out, but it was painful. At times I was crying out of pain but just seeing someone that you love and who believes in you was overwhelming when you're doing something you think is impossible. I knew if I didn't stop it would hold. Keep the motion Joy, slow and steady; for 26.2 miles. At these pre-determined spots, my husband would record short video clips of me and post them on social media. There were friends and family that were cheering me on. As he posted these clips, my phone was beeping with texts and I knew they were encouraging words from people who loved me. I couldn't read them but I knew they were there, and that was enough for me to keep moving, to not quit.

By the time I reached the twenty-mile mark, I had not stopped moving for the entirety. I knew things were going downhill for me so I started preparing myself. It was the last leg, and I had reached the maximum number of miles I had ever run in training. My husband pulled alongside me and asked if I was okay and I assured him I was. Encouraging him to go on ahead and to skip the last spot was necessary for me finishing this. With only six more miles to go, I told him I would see him at the finish. I smiled at him with my brave face and thumbs up as he drove away; I knew that I needed to do this on my own. If he were there and as I became more injured than I was, I knew that he would have had a hard time watching me in that much pain. And in the same turn, I would also have an out if he was there. So I set my mind on God, my only sustainer and I buckled down in prayer. As I neared mile-twenty-two things started to break down: My mind, my spirit, my thoughts, and my leg... my everything. This was tough, even for me. I'm stubborn; I finish what I start, and I would not let this be a moment of regret.

Just before mile-twenty-four, I had run out of water and I was feeling dizzy. A biker in the race was on the course and asked if I was okay and encouraged me to make it to the final water stop just up the way. But just before I reached it, I stopped. In the moment of all moments, I knew I blew it. This is like that moment that you hit send on an email and immediately you want to take it back. So you hold the key down, not wanting to lift it up because you realize it's going to send the moment you release your finger. Well, that was me. My leg seized and locked up and I now had a wooden leg.

As I was internally kicking myself, I stood in the road and looked up. I had hoped that God saw me, that He could see little 'ole me standing in the road and hear my cry.

"It's all you," I said. *This has to be you!* I walked to the station just a ways up. Boom! The other leg went out. I now was a stick-man walking. I was in tears at this point and the military cadet standing in the intersection looked at me as if he understood my pain and my perseverance. As he kept his eyes straight ahead, he nodded to me with a slight tilt of his head, as if to encourage me to push through the pain. In that moment, not only did I relate to what these men and women of service do every day, but saw that he appreciated and respected my not giving up. The tears streaming down my face were uncontrollable and under the circumstances where most would give up, that cadet and I had a moment of understanding that only two sustainers could understand. He had encouraged me with just a tilt of his head and I will never forget that. He was my great blue heron that day standing in the road. I grabbed a banana off the table, filled my water bottle, took out my last Advil and knew I had to do this thing, this last two miles. As I began to run, my legs were wobbling and I could not get them under control. It wasn't pretty nor was it pleasant. Runners passed me as I struggled and I knew that God had placed me in this very spot for a reason.

It was in this moment where I felt as if everything stopped and was quiet and I stood once again alone in the stillness. Or maybe I was delirious at this point and was on the verge of passing out, but what I know is that He saw my determination, He saw the lengths that I would go, He saw the discipline that I displayed and He saw my faith in Him. He saw my eyes set on him, looking up where my only hope in finishing this thing was His call. As I stood on the corner looking in the direction of where I was to go, I knew that only He could provide me the balance, the strength and the will to endure this pain. I prayed for Him to just bring my legs in, tuck them under me and I would do the rest. It was only seconds that I realized I was running. Maybe not gracefully but I was moving; only on one good leg, but it was working. I looked down several times during those last two miles to even see if I was even running. I couldn't feel them at this point and knew that it would compromise my good or less injured leg. It was a mindset and will to survive, is the only way I can describe it.

As I continued to run, people were sitting outside eating lunch at local restaurants, window shopping and just hanging out. I'm sure I looked ridiculous to them, but in that moment I didn't care. It was just me and Him. At that moment my eyes were on Him and I knew He had me. I'm sure passersby had no idea what was happening in the road with me and *to* me. I was alone with God and unbeknownst to the spectators, the Lord Almighty just passed by on Palafox Street that day carrying his child to the finish line.

His perfect love will always override anything that you feel defeats you.

Thinking back on a time when you pushed yourself to the limits of what you could endure, where quitting was not an option, and you had to relinquish all control; whatever it was, you were not alone. His perfect love will always override anything that defeats you. To believe in yourself that you can persevere with His great power, is where faith—raw faith—happens. And where raw faith is present, there lies perseverance. In being purposeful and intentional leads to life changes and in having a forward movement. This experience was a test of my faith and I grew to understand that all things ARE possible with Him. It was, as I describe, being tucked in ever so tightly and pressed in His arms that the moments following felt like it was just the two of us. Making the final turn, I saw it. The finish line... up ahead. So that is where the last .2 miles of a marathon comes in.

CHAPTER 16

Big things come in small packages.

This is where most people quit in life, the final .2 "miles" of their journey. In most situations in our lives, this is where it gets hard. This is where we often choose the easier way. It is in the smallest, finest details of life that make all the difference. This is where you're tempted to compromise everything that you've told yourself about who you are and what you can or cannot achieve.

Who are you? You ask yourself, "Am I a quitter, a finisher, or a fighter?" You want to slow down but you see it, the home stretch, and the possibility of finishing what seems impossible. It's the end of all the hard work and training; it's saying that you CAN and you did. As you near the end, the final pages of the chapter which you thought was impossible, just up ahead and you dig deep and run with all your might. The final burst of everything you have within you and you give it all you have left; that's life! That's living with undeniable faith.

> *Living life in the final bursts are life changers.*

Those final bursts toward completion are the life changing moments. Do not quit and do not slow down and please, please do not miss them. That is the enemy telling you that you can't and that you are nothing. This is where fear sets in because you might just do it! These are the important decisions, life changing moments that are game-changers.

One of my favorite quotes is "Life begins at the end of your comfort zone." Pushing through what is uncomfortable and living your life is the moments that change WHO you are and WHO you are meant to be.

I remember two police officers standing on the last intersection that I was to cross and everything seemed to be in slow motion at this point. They were cheering me on, clapping with smiles that paved the final steps of this masterpiece He was creating right before my eyes.

One officer pointed up ahead and said to me, "There it is... go get it!" It's as if God gave me that final push, words of encouragement from strangers and the willingness to never quit that brought everything from the prior sixteen weeks of preparation to this one moment. All the steps I'd taken to this point ran like a film strip through my mind; signing up for the race, the early morning trainings, the hundreds of miles, the sweat, blood and tears. They all ran together in fast motion to lead to this one specific moment. And then it slowed to the present moment and I had to decide: quit or finish. I was tested on the distance I would go, the discipline I'd summon. In that one moment of love I knew that this beautiful ending planned just for me. I had proven to myself (God already knew) I'd go the extra mile in whatever He has planned.

Lean into your faith and face your fears head-on; it brings moments of greatness. This, my friend, is not being *able* to quit. You don't know *how* to quit when God is on your side.

And yet it seemed like forever these .2 miles to reach the end... the period on my final sentence of this journey. The final ".2" of most life-changing decisions seems to last forever. Believe in His timing; believe that going the extra mile makes the difference between quitting or finishing.

On this home stretch up ahead He provided this bright light, my trainer, my pacer who led me through the sixteen weeks of training. My group had finished an hour prior, but she had waited to see me finish, encouraging me 'til the end, as if God knew I would need it. This was the person who trained me, ran countless miles with me, and encouraged me for sixteen weeks by telling me that I could do it. This was the final demonstration of the love that God had for me in finishing this challenge. She ran with me to the barriers and she too, then said, "Go get your finish."

And as I neared, I heard my name, "Joy Schulz, a finisher, a marathoner" and in that same moment, I heard, "a child of God."

Simply by being a child of God, you are a finisher, you are a sustainer and you are unstoppable, even when it's hard. When you finish and cross that line, it's like you're in slow motion. These are the moments when you know that you've forgotten how to quit. It's just not in you to give up and believe you can't do something. The moment you believe nothing is impossible, it's not. Let's face it... I didn't do that on my own! There is no way that a fifty-year-old with two blown out IT bands ran 26.2 miles. I also believe it was the moment that I leaned so far into God's love that I surrendered myself and everything I had. That is the very same moment He took over... for me; little ole me standing in the road.

It was an experience I will never forget where He had left an impression on my heart and where I had left an impression in His arms of the weight of Him carrying me. It was where God truly—I mean without a doubt—met me on the pavement and allowed me to continue on. I demonstrated to myself that "where there's a will, there's a way." There is only one way, this I know. Looking back, I see Him all along the way of the training. The challenging of myself, the injury, the willingness to continue, the test of will, the test of faith, the surrendering, the sending my husband on, the military officer, the police officers, and then my pacer at the finish encouraging me all along the way. They were all my smooth stones in which I used to conquer this Goliath. But the most used weapon of all was having faith to defeat this giant.

> *He sees little 'ole you standing in the road.*

Following that experience, I have a true understanding of His purpose for me and I will go on whatever path He leads. When He responded to me, "Teacher of what?" I finally began to see the true meaning of my journey.

Questions for Your Journey

- ❖ You don't have to run a marathon to meet God on the road. Describe a moment of "stillness" where you knew He was present.

- ❖ What is a ".2" moment that you've been procrastinating on in finishing? What steps can you take to push through the fear and make it happen?

FREE WILL

"No temptation has overtaken you except what is common to mankind. And God is faithful; he will not let you be tempted beyond what you can bear. But when you are tempted, he will also provide a way out so that you can endure it."
~ 1 Corinthians 10:13

CHAPTER 17

You are the light of the world.

Existing in our little world where we can do something outstanding to make a difference simply by doing something completely selfless is a gift. It's a decision on your part every day to do so—that is called free will.

Free will began in the Garden of Eden, where the stage was set to decipher between right and wrong. These choices come with accountability. It is where the "self" has choices and it is those choices that determine our future. When making these choices, it all comes down to what is in our heart. The heart reflects what behaviors we demonstrate to the world, thus showing free will. There it is again... free will. What does that mean?

"Free" means that you are not under the control of anyone else. "Will" is about choosing your own actions. So being given "free will" is the freedom to do whatever you want. So what will it be, your will or God's will? It's so simple, yet we make it so hard.

What is the will of God?

There are twenty-two Scriptures that talk about the will of God for our lives. I believe the one that is most fitting for my life is in Thessalonians 5:18, "Give thanks in all circumstances; for this is God's will for you in Christ Jesus."; *In ALL circumstances*. Sometimes that's a hard one for me, for you, for everyone who has battled in our lives. But the reward comes when we get to that undeniable belief and trust in God.

I'm striving to be raw in faith, but I have to admit it's hard. So hard that I'm running it down like my life depends on it. Not the end of my life here on earth, but spiritually. During those times, He takes us by the hand and walks us through every situation and gets us to the other side.

Often we'd like to erase it from our minds, never talk or think about it again. But it is those tough moments in life where we can be a true testament to someone else going through the same situation; the same ugly moment that you are so desperately trying to forget. Running away from it and pretending it never happened is what we do best. By forgetting the ugliness, we take all that God walked us through and make it as if it didn't matter, as if it never happened… or what I call, "wasting a save." What's the point in making the journey if you can't share the story and possibly be a light to someone else? Maybe that's the whole purpose of this moment, even the one you're in right now, to use your experiences to help another.

In Matthew 5:14-16, "You are the light of the world. A town built on a hill cannot be hidden. Neither do people light a lamp and put it under a bowl. Instead they put it on its stand, and it gives light to everyone in the house. In the same way, let your light shine before others, that they may see your good deeds and glorify your Father in heaven."

Be the light for someone else.

It's like that moment when you're talking to someone and they talk about what's going on in their life. It's a mess and you then realize that you have a footprint in that mess. Meaning, you've been there and done that. You think to yourself that you are so grateful to be through it, past it and, having moved beyond it, and are trying to forget it. But here it is, staring you in the face. Here is someone, on the familiar path in the moments where God gave mercy and grace to you in your life.

I always imagine this could be one of those moments in a movie when the camera freezes and the actor turns to the camera to address the viewer. I then envision myself turning to God and saying, "This is it, right? This is the moment that you're using me, why you gave me that save, to help this person, right?" So here goes! Let's be humbled, let's take out the ugly and let's use it for good.

The producer calls "Action," the cameras click on and here we go. And then I say, "I know and understand what you're going through." I share my story; the testimony given, hoping to share my faith to that person in their valley moment. That's a thought... What if a difference can be made by living your life out through Christ where you impacted someone else; someone that needed to witness your life, to hear about your ugly moments of truth? The options are endless... every day... and we somehow miss them. It's about being obedient, humble and eager for His will in our lives, this free will that is given.

CHAPTER 18

What's your word?

So what's your word? For the past few years I've asked God for a word to sum up my coming year. It can be a word of something that I need to work on or a word that resonates with me for many other reasons. It can be anything.

So on January 1, 2016 I asked for my word and—boom—He delivered it… transparent. My immediate response: Nope... I want another one. A few days later I asked, "No really, let's try again. What's my word?" Transparent. So, transparent it was. And it ended up being an exhausting and humbling year.

[What happens if you don't get what you want?]

Mostly, I'm a private person. That's why me writing this book is one of the hardest things I've ever done. I've read it countless times and always question whether it's worth the read. But within this year of transparency God placed people on my path to which I revealed my moments of truth, and He used them for good. Cameras, lights, and go! The outpouring of honesty from people's response when I was transparent almost became comical. I realized that by witnessing their struggles, I could help them. If sharing my ugly moments could impact someone else's detour and get them on the path again, then mission accomplished. By giving me the confidence to extend my hand to others in their valleys, He gave me a newfound strength that helped to form this warrior inside. Hence, here I am writing this in hoping to reach you in your ugly moments. Or a victory, but regardless, connecting our stories or paths for His good.

It was through this transformation that I began to see things differently. Everything became clearer and more defined through this transparency thing. I began to see God in everything. He was teaching me that He is everywhere giving us "saves" and it is our responsibility—me and you—to share these moments and help someone else to the other side. By being the light, His hands and feet, He gives us opportunities to share hope with someone else.

The year 2017 the word I was given was "*acceptance*." I believe accepting life's challenges, taking them on instead of living in denial, allows us to move forward. To actively participate in the word acceptance would mean to accept or consent to what is being offered. There were many things that I had to accept in my life during this year and by training me in this word, I began to grow. To accept what is to come or what is not, is accepting what He gives us.

Each day we fill our lives with distractions that keep us from appreciating the gifts that surround us. The sunrises and sunsets are painted canvases that I used to miss. I mean I would notice them, but not see them for what they are. We take them for granted, not giving much thought to the beauty He is creating around us. In Psalms 19:1, it reads, "The heavens declare the glory of God; the skies proclaim the work of his hands." God reaches us through nature. He speaks to us through beauty in the most common of things. In today's world, we don't take a moment out of the day to just breathe, give ourselves a break, and appreciate those little things.

Have you ever just looked at the detail of a butterfly? The next time one flutters by, consider how it's able to fly with its tissue paper wings. The delicacy of its wings somehow seems impossible; or how about a bumblebee? I once researched the flight of a bumblebee and learned that its body size and wing span should make it impossible to fly. Look it up; it's a miracle. I don't want to miss a single moment of what God has put in front of me.

It's time to slow down, take a deep breath and sit in it... sit in the grace and mercy of each day. Sit and have patience in His timing and wait for His leading. Appreciate every little thing around us, be purposeful in our actions, confident in our stride, and fearless in our belief of who we are and who we are to meant to become. Because that person you *want* to be but never thought you could be, is God's plan for you. It starts with a thought that nudges you toward your path. But then the doubt sets in and you stop. Don't stop before the last ".2" and redirect your steps toward your dreams. If we all just begin to ***BE*** who we want to be, I believe we will become the people we are meant to be. First we have to quiet the noise of life and be still. Stillness and waiting on the Lord is what I learned to accept in preparation for this next year of focus.

Begin to be who you want to be and you will eventually become the person you are meant to be.

In Matthew 22:37, "Jesus replied, 'Love the Lord your God with all your heart and with all your soul and with your entire mind.'" It's called free will because we get to make a choice to live our lives for His will or for our own. This freedom is a gift from God. It allows us to *choose* to love Him because we get to, not because we have to. By believing that you can, and then you will, every time.

My word for 2018 was "*focus*." Wow, that's funny. For the past ten years it may seem that I have been unfocused. But with everything that has happened to our family, what appeared to be chaos, was a controlled chaos during a year of focus for us. This has been a journey of not settling, not doing the norm and waiting on His timing. This last year has been a year of not doing what everyone thinks I should do or should not be doing. It has been a time of doing what I had to do to take care of my family while still preserving His will for me. It has been a path of tapping into my creative space and exploring the "what if" moments that He's placed in my heart. So my word "focus" for this year was fitting. This year God brought me to a standstill, where I now had all the tools He provided to move forward.

It was during this year, the first six months I stood still; the quiet was deafening. It was a time of reflection to examine and decide which way to go. I'd just completed my second year of my jewelry. This business has focused me on His vision and I have to admit I was not sure at times what I was doing. The time and energy that I gave focused me and created a space where my time with Him grew. But the further I dove into this business, the more I was able to encourage women I didn't even know. Encouraging women to be bold in their faith and just BE who they want to be was empowering and was monumental.

The last six months of that year I ended my job at the church and came out of my desert time that had "feet in the sand" moments. Sometimes we stay or sit too long in places that eventually make us complacent. And that's on you and I for letting it become a refuge for too long. So I stood up, shook the sand off my feet and entered a new season. And I am now finishing this, this book that has given me the opportunity to work through my stuff. My junk, the moments in life that you wish to forget but also the ones that reflect your journey. In releasing these moments, sharing them, giving testimony, not wasting His saves, I will take this opportunity and run with it: focused.

The year is now 2019 and my word is "look". So now that I have my feet placed in the right direction, I will *look* to Him about every decision before taking a step. I will *look* to Him for counsel with every vision given. And I will *look* to Him for my direction on my path and will not make a move on my own. I feel, at times, like I'm running a race. It's like I'm one of the horses at the Kentucky Derby, in the gate, anxiously waiting for the signal. In the *looking* part of this year, it was as though blinders were put on me to keep my attention on the things that move me forward, straight ahead.

Blinders are used for horses, especially those who tend to lose concentration, to keep them from looking beside or behind them; keeping them focused on the track ahead. Isn't life the same, we are constantly looking back in our rearview mirror, and reliving our past, letting that determine our steps? We should only look back at our past to grow from it and keep our blinders on to live in the present and continue to move forward. That's where you find me… waiting for the signal to move.

So what's your word? The word given to you, many times, is not the word you want. It's kind of like when you muster up the courage to give something up for Lent. When everyone is spouting off something they will give up or add to their life for the next 40 days and the first thing that springs to mind is the unthinkable, something you can't, or think you can't live without; like candy for me.

I'll admit I was in love with candy. I had candy hidden all over—in my car, purse, house, office, in every nook and cranny—and ate it all day long. So here I was faced with, "What will be a challenge for my thoughts to revert to Christ when I think I can't live without something?" Well, that first thing you think of, that's it. You try to back-pedal, "Well, whoa! Wait a minute… Not that!" And you come up with something simple like toast instead. Well, I have to say, after giving up candy for two years, I now do not eat candy. It's not like you can cheat and sit in a closet away from your family and friends; its God and He sees you in the closet.

So the same is true for your word, when asking for a word that would help give you a clear vision for your new year and what to work on. Take it in stride and live each day toward that word, as hard as it is. I have found that, while sometimes hard, it always brings good and gives us an opportunity to move forward.

QUESTIONS FOR YOUR JOURNEY

❖ What's your word? Sit and pray for it and accept what's given… it has meaning to your future.

CHAPTER 19

Don't let fear win.

Opportunity is one of my favorite words. Opportunities move us forward. They're all around us, but often when we are presented with one, we tend to blow it. We talk ourselves out of seizing it. We get distracted and when we look back, it's gone. Just like that. How can we grow in the ability to notice opportunity when it comes?

Opportunity is normally accompanied by a fellow named "fear." Fear makes you doubt your adequacy. Fear allows you to stop dead in your tracks in the middle of the path that your Heavenly Father has laid before you. Fear is sometimes very comforting because it allows you to stay in your quiet, comfortable stagnant state which requires no real effort and is familiar. So you sit and watch opportunities go by, believing that they were meant for someone else more qualified and you wait on the next one. What if.... what if that opportunity is for YOU! What if God's purpose was within the walls of that very thing that would propel you forward into becoming who you are meant to be?

[*Opportunity is normally accompanied by a fellow name "fear".*]

That's a good question, who are you meant to be? Well, let's think about that. What are your passions in life? What gets your goat and *what does that mean*? What fires you up so bad that you can't stand it? What keeps you up at night with thoughts of how you could change that very thing to make this world a little bit better? And lastly, what are your talents...what are you good at? What has God given you naturally, that comes easily to you?

What fires you up? What keeps you up at night? What are your gifts and talents?

After pondering these questions, you may get a glimpse of your *purpose*. Your purpose, isn't that what we are all after in the end? You hear about the word "purpose" and you search and wonder your whole life if you'll find it, or have found it, or are you close to finding it, or maybe that you just don't have one. We tell our kids to find their purpose in life with no real instructions. Imagine a ten-year-old and the stress of having to comprehend, much less worry about this big question... What is my purpose? God knows your purpose and if you allow Him to work in you from the inside out, the destination becomes much clearer.

This means giving up control—wait, did I just say that? Me—the one that God has chased down, played tug-of-war with, and still continues to reveal my purpose?

This reminds me of Solomon. God offered him anything he wanted, but he only asked for one thing: wisdom. So God made him the wisest man alive and it was through that wisdom that he found his purpose. God was so pleased that Solomon did not ask for materialistic items that he gave him great wealth and influence as well.

When my kids are worried about taking a test, I always tell them to pray for wisdom, not the answers. God knows the answers, but in giving you wisdom, it will satisfy you with the results. Solomon was wise, and thus knew how to apply his knowledge to lead a blessed and long life. For most of us, we may have to be re-routed or take a detour many times, but if we keep hanging on to that hope that he puts inside us and seek His wisdom in our journey, just as Solomon did, we can have a blessed life. He was not perfect by any means, but it was through his wisdom that he could help and lead others.

Does remaining in control of your life mean that you will find happiness? We often act like it does, when in reality, it's giving *up* that control that leads to freedom and blessing. It's like when you go to church and you feel that alter call to "lay it all down." Mustering up the strength and courage to rise from your seat and walk that aisle as if you have lead in your heels, you make your way down to the altar. Kneeling with all your emotions high, you pray. You become emotional because the very thing that you're laying down is something that you've grown attached to. It's comfortable and how will you live a life without it? But you feel the music and you prepare the release of whatever you're giving up to God for Him to deal with, for Him to take and set you free. So now kneeling at the altar and feeling much better with a lighter load than when you arrived, you rise and turn, but just before you leave you snatch those very things right back and return to your seat. You exit the doors of the church and wonder why the days seem the same and the concerns are still there. You're thinking, "Is God not hearing me?" Give...it...up! If you take the opportunities placed before you, surrender control to His wisdom, and use your talents, I believe you'll find the purpose of your life.

As I sit here, I'm trying to recall a time when I didn't take on an opportunity. For someone like me, change is a good thing. Someone I respect once told me to just find one thing, just one thing in life and just do that. It was in a moment when I had turned my feet in a direction that I thought was my path. Boom! And those words blocked my path. I sat down in my doubt. It was said in such a way that conjured up a negative connotation, at least to me. I interpreted this person as saying I had no direction or qualities to offer. That experience became a permanent barrier in my life for several years. Those words triggered the doubt and insecurities within me and sent me in a downward spiral.

I felt I was not qualified to do the "one thing" I thought I was supposed to do and I let the fear of failure win. I did what most of us do. I was paralyzed and did nothing. I coveted quiet places, and I did not move forward or grow in that area for two years.

For those who know me, this was not a typical behavior for me. I am active and thrive with change. I love change! It moves me; it challenges me and it is who I am.

It took me hearing a podcast of someone speaking about this very thing for me to finally come out of my paralysis. The speaker related to me and struggled with similar fears. In that moment I realized that I *was* qualified. I had let someone else's doubt in my abilities define me, given in to the feeling of inadequacy. And maybe for the person who'd questioned me, my way of living appeared to them to be "unfocused." Maybe I seemed irresponsible or unstable to them. But, for a person like me, movement, being challenged, being moved by something worth being moved by is the life in which I thrive.

I will never again sit still and just let life happen. I know that about myself now. To me that would be a life not worth living; to be stagnant, not grow, get lost in the monotony seems incomprehensible to me. I am enlivened by creating opportunities to help people improve and challenging them to be a better version of themselves. And then I move on. Once I realized that, it set me free!

Many, many years ago, I had a dear friend tell me he interpreted my spirit the same as a "*sprite*." A sprite is a mythical creature or fairy, also known as a spirit or soul. He would say that I pop into people's lives and enrich them by giving them what they need, and then move on as fast as I arrived. And so it is.

So what moves you? What motivates you to be a better version of yourself? Is it having a stable job and just doing that? If that's it, then do that. If it's moving upward in a constant learning pattern and motion, then do that. Do what is in your heart and never allow the opinions of others to derail you. That's on you, not them.

Our time here on earth is not for ourselves but for His purpose only. Life on earth is not IT; it's merely the means to an end. Don't waste it; don't live for yesterday or tomorrow, but only for today and what you can contribute that will impact eternity. Ask yourself, "What can I do today to move myself forward and be who He has called me to be?" When fear sneaks in, I say that it means that something good is about to happen. It could be a decision or action that just might mean something. It means that you might just light a fire in the path of your future. I love the quote from Helen Keller, "A bend in the road is not the end of the road unless you fail to make the turn." The thing you are fearful of could be the very thing that changes the course of your life. Sometimes changing your mind can change who

"A bend in the road is not the end of the road unless you fail to make the turn."

you become. And don't worry; I change my mind all the time. Every day you are one decision away from changing your path. You have the ability to change... today.

In 1 Corinthians 10:13 it reads, "No temptation has overtaken you except what is common to mankind. And God is faithful; He will not let you be tempted beyond what you can bear. But when you are tempted He will also provide a way out so that you can endure it." That is great news! There are at least two paths for every decision you make, every day! It's your life, so live it and swim in the depths of being courageous.

Another word that is similar to courageous is the word *Bold*. Similar words to bold are to be *daring* in the face of opposition; *brave* when you are fearful; and *fearless* in your faith. And sometimes that might mean a change. Maybe if you continue to push through the fear, and do it anyway, you might find that you ARE qualified, you ARE glorified and you ARE loved.

Well, I do know this. Fear is not of God. Fear has nothing to do with God. So what is fear? To me, fear is the enemy holding you for ransom, holding on to you with a tight grip and a clenched fist. Fear is what will hold you back from yourself and from ever doing anything pleasing to God. The enemy does not want you to succeed. The enemy does not want you to be confident, mighty, or audacious. But if you push through it and go for it— yes, go for it in faith—He will be there waiting for you anticipating your next leg of your journey. With fear winning, you will have missed an opportunity to explode to the next chapter of your life.

Fear has nothing to do with God.

This brings me to a moment where I was giving in to fear—not for me but one of my sons. My son, at a young age, was interested in music. He started with the keyboard and eventually moved on to the guitar. It was in his middle school years that our worship leader embraced his interest in music and helped set him on this path.

The Sunday morning of his first time playing for our congregation he woke up that morning and said that he couldn't do it; he was afraid. As I talked with him about it I reminded him that God was so pleased in his leading worship today but on the other side of the spectrum was a fellow named Satan who would like only for him to fail. This was one of those moments where fear was getting him off track. It was making him stop and question his ability to make judgement calls about himself and miss the moment that may just set him apart. I encouraged him to push through the fear.

So, he stepped on that stage and he did it! He blazed a trail into his future. After that fearful day, he saw a light of a gift that was given. He went on to play throughout middle school, high school, college, and even on mission trips. He led worship at Fellowship of Christian Athletes gatherings during his high school years; going on mission trips and taking part in youth rallies in the middle of cities that needed to hear the message. He joined a band at a church during college and was a part of an incredible Christian group that then became some of his best friends. And it all hinged on that one day, that one day where he was courageous, daring, brave and fearless. God took him places because of his faith and in the pursuit of sharing it.

Since then we have talked about that day. The "what if" he hadn't played that day; would he have continued? All the occasions of leading worship and all the friends that he found that might not have happened. It is by pushing through the fearful moments by shear will that the magic happens. And if you don't, you will have let the enemy win and as God as my witness, that is the last thing I ever want to happen in my life.

I have been afraid of failure my entire life but today when I feel fear, I approach it head on with the power of God that lives within me. It challenges me in my faith and willingness to submit to His will and believe that He's got this. Do I still falter? Sure, but I get back up and try again. So go ahead... give Satan the finger. It was during a past Bible study that someone said that Satan can only hear your words and see your actions; and that God is the only one that can hear your thoughts. I pray quietly, at times when unsure. I do all the time when he's hot on my trail and nothing gives me more pleasure than that. I can only show through words or actions. So that is what I do; I give him the finger and say, "Not today!"

I've had many fears in my younger years and I've let others control my thoughts and desires that I have had in this world. I've missed it many times, given in to fear and not pushed through, but still, God has not given up on me yet. His pace was always in stride with mine, even when

I felt alone. He kept up with me and never left my side. Even when I couldn't see it, He did. I know that now when looking back and feel, although I've taken the long way around, I'm on the path with Him now and I trust His steps for me. I've always been the captain of my vessel with an "I've got this" attitude and believed I was the wind in my own sails. But as I've trusted in Him and allowed Him to work from the inside out, He has become my wind and compass setting the direction I follow. And He wants to do this with you. He wants to be *your everything*; the wind in your sails and the rudder keeping you on course.

His pace is always in stride with yours and He never leaves your side.

Sometimes we can't see it and sometimes we're uncomfortable in what we see. The possibilities to be all that He knows we can be are staggering. The answer may be "no" or "not yet" and we struggle to accept that. But to believe that where He's sending you and me might involve the answer "no" because it's what's best for that time or season in our lives, leads to moments where true and fierce faith comes in. It is only when we look back and see the design in how the moments of our lives have been woven together and how each has been a stepping stone for the one before, that we experience his love and plan for our lives.

Questions for Your Journey

- What was a hard "No" in your past that at the time it felt like the end?

- How do you see that "No" being a positive in your life today?

CHAPTER 20

The gift of opportunity.

Opportunity is one of those things that can be hard to see. Recognizing an opportunity when faced with one is difficult. The opportunity of me going back to school was huge and led me to here, writing this. Sometimes you might do something and wonder how you got to this place, doing this one thing and how does this fit in with what "I" want to do? But I have now learned that we are not in control and I have become more relaxed with this thing I call "sitting in it."

That's what I do now. I just sit in it when I don't know what to do. What is "it"? "It" is life. It's taking time to figure it out and wait on your next move. By "sitting still," I'm more self-aware and able to truly listen. No matter what I'm doing or what job I'm in, it's all a part of the plan and purpose for that particular season of my life. Each ingredient is just as important as the next.

So wherever you find yourself in your life, even if it's not what you planned or want, just appreciate the learning moments and the people you meet. He has planned for you to be right where you are, molding and shaping you into this marvelous creation. But what if where you are in life, let's call it a detour, has nothing to do with you. What if your detour has everything to do with someone else? By changing the course of their life, saying what they needed to hear, or having them be a witness to your life.

> *What if your detour had to do with someone else in changing their course?*

In Philippians 2:3 it states that, "For it is God who works in you to will and to act in order to fulfill his purpose." Just imagining that God would use me or you to fulfill his purpose in others is humbling and an honor. Being open to this thought blows my mind.

I tried hard to display the perfect life on the outside, but inside the walls of this little box was a mess. I can remember back when going to church, attempting to do well was a "check the box" way of living that left me empty and always searching for more. I would fill my days with tasks, anything that made me feel whole and accomplished, never feeling fulfilled or satisfied.

Getting things done is what I do well. From start to finish, no matter what the task, I won't give up until it's done. My days became weeks and my weeks rolled into months and before you knew it, I was too busy to see past the appointments, schedules, and things I had to organize for other people. I didn't have time for me or my family, and most of all, not enough time for God. The enemy likes to do that ever so quietly. He doesn't rush in and make a grand entrance. He permeates every nook and cranny in your life until you no longer have time for anything else. But I'm getting things done, right? The enemy will lead you to believe that if you're not busy, you're not doing enough. Whatever it takes, hear me when I say this.... you are never too busy for God. And this brings me to Martha.

In the gospel of Luke, Jesus and his disciples were traveling through a village and stopped at the home of Martha and her sister Mary. Martha scurried about, overwhelmed by all the preparations for their guests. She was much more worried about getting the meal together than spending time with the guest of honor, Jesus. She was upset with Mary, who sat at Jesus' feet listening to his teachings instead of helping her. In Matthew 4:4 Jesus says, "Man shall not live on bread alone, but by every word of God." Martha told Jesus that it upset her that Mary was not helping. But Jesus was more pleased that Mary spent time with him, making Him a priority. Isn't that the truth! The time He spends waiting and directing our steps, and yet the thought of spending quiet time, even five minutes of reading the Word, keeping up with your daily devotional, or in taking a moment to praise Him, seems like another task to schedule into your day. My time with God starts the moment I open my eyes. He is the first thing I think about and the last as I give thanks for at the end of the day. I ask Him daily, “What are we going to do today?” I praise Him for the opportunities of the day. That didn’t just happen, that took discipline at first. In saying that I’ve had many opportunities, I have. I’ve blown most of them but I feel as if the detours got me back on track. I may be late for this party called life, but the journey has taught me to value my time appropriately and be intentional with it.

So this leads me to a time in my life where opportunities were all around me, where grace and mercy were given and where I recognized the difference.

Questions for Your Journey

- ❖ Is there an ugly moment that you feel you "would-have-should have" about? What steps can you take to not wasting that "save" the next time?

- ❖ Is there a moment in life where you let the words of others deflect your steps? How can you get back on the path?

GRACE

But he said to me, "My grace is sufficient to you, for my power is made perfect in weakness." Therefore, I will boast all the more gladly about my weaknesses, so that Christ's power may rest on me.
-2 Corinthians 12:8

CHAPTER 21

Are grace and mercy the same?

So what is grace? Grace and mercy always seem to be used together but they both hold a much different meaning. Grace has been one of the most important or main reasons for the Bible. God's grace is His love given when we don't deserve it. Whereas in mercy, God withholds judgement we deserve and does not punish us for our sins. His *grace* allows Him to have compassion ***for*** us despite our sinful nature and His *mercy* does not punish us *in* our sinful nature.

I remember reading the Bible for the first time cover to cover, starting with page one. I began in the Old Testament and by the end of it I began to feel as if I understood what grace was and I was a little nervous. There were moments that, as a new Christian, were brow-sweating moments. As I began the New Testament, I felt as if there was a more loving and patient God. I've talked at great length with many people about this grace-giving God, and the question often arose regarding whether the God of the Old and New Testament were different. But when you dig more deeply, you see a loving God who deals with sin in the same manner throughout the Bible, in both testaments. It describes Him as an "unchanging" God and his grace and mercy are exhibited throughout Scripture. He called people into a relationship with Him and showed great mercy to those who didn't deserve it.

In the Old Testament you can find in Psalm 86:5, "You, Lord, are forgiving and good, abounding in love to all who call to you." And in the New Testament in John 3:16, "For God so loved the world that he gave his one and only Son, that whoever believes in him shall not perish but have eternal life." That is a true, unchanging and just God who wants only to be our Father in Heaven.

The more I learned I began to wake from this sleep and began to understand what all this was all about. So, God has given me grace and mercy— absolutely. He extends that to all of us and yet we somehow still miss it, and goes unnoticed.

If you wrote a list of all the opportunities that came your way, leading up to today, how would that look? How did those defining moments in the jobs you've had and the people you have met along the way, all work together to land you where you are today? While reflecting over your timeline, here is a view of mine leading up to a monumental moment in my life where grace was leading me to the place I am today.

CHAPTER 22

Making a timeline.

My life leading up to college graduation consisted of various jobs I performed just to get by. They weren't lifelong dream jobs I felt called to; they were a place to go and provided financial security for my family. I appreciated all the opportunities to better my family and support them, but in the big scheme of things in living out my purpose, nothing quite hit the mark. I had a high school diploma, and I spent most of my life in sales and administrative positions in where I served others. I never felt satisfied or fulfilled and was always looking for something else, something more. But as I look back on all the various positions that I've had, I now see how they were all a part of this big picture of where I am standing today. I needed every detail of each position in preparation of this moment in my life of feeling confident in where He is leading me. In sales, I learned the art of listening and understanding one's needs. While in administrative/management positions, I learned organizational skills and equipping others in what they needed to succeed. Still as a realtor, I've learned to multi-task, prioritize and am thorough in the task. It's about culminating relationships and nurturing people in their new beginnings. While at American Cancer Society as a community rep, I learned the need to be aware of those around me; to understand that everyone has a story and be available to walk through the hard stuff with people as a witness to their true faith.

In my college years, I learned about endurance, perseverance, and never giving up… those late-night essays! Then working at my church as hospitality director, I served a large congregation and provided support and service to those around me by making them feel welcome and loved on. It was like the final cherry on top of this excellent sundae of my life He was creating. He now had me in the venue where it would be pieced together for His good.

In my quest to obtain my college degree, grace was given time and time again. Grace and mercy met me head-on. But let's back up to the moment I decided to go back to school and it will become clear.

CHAPTER 23

Dare you to move.

It was a rainy day, the year was 2011, and I was working 50+ hours a week at my current job, missing every soccer game and financially strapped. These were the "praise you in the storm" days. The day prior, I had picked up our tax information from our CPA and things looked bleak. I had mentioned in conversation at one time with her that I had always wanted to be a teacher. But the chance of that ever happening was next to impossible. Remember that word "impossible," meaning never to try. Well, that was me.

Unbeknownst to me, she had cut out a newspaper clipping about education degrees from a local community college. I was walking away, she said, "Oh, wait, I have something for you." She handed me the small clipping. I never imagined that single clipping would take me on this amazing journey to where I am now. The smallest moments can bring the most impact. It was a clipping about getting certified as a teacher with the contact information of whom to call. I thanked her and sat in my car and just cried. This just sounded impossible to me; we didn't have the funds, and I didn't have the time with my current job. I thought about it for days, saying nothing to anyone.

> *At times, it is the smallest moments that are the most impactful.*

Enter now the current rainy day, sitting outside my work. By this time, my radio was always tuned to KLOVE, and I found great encouragement in the music. It was through these songs that God reached me and I found refuge in them. I wasn't opening my Bible, I wasn't attending any Bible studies, and I wasn't talking with anyone about God. Who has the time, right? I mean, I can't even make it home for dinner or see a game. Let's just say my priorities were not in line with the big picture and the enemy had my day-planner. I was only doing what I thought I had to in order to survive every day.

So a song came on the radio that dared me to move. I remembered the game called *Truth or Dare* from childhood. Neither choice is comfortable, but you're forced to make one. Are you to be truthful in your situation or will you take the dare and test your mettle? Telling the truth is so much harder than getting through a dare. Telling the truth reveals our heart, our fears, and exposes us to potential hurt. So, a dare it is! It was in this moment that I felt God's nudge and He dared me to call this woman from the education department and make a move. After all these years of wanting to be this person in education, but never following through, it seemed scary. What if I can't, what if I fail, what if…? These are the words I heard like a broken record. But, what if I *did*?

I called the very next day and set up a meeting about going back to school. About following a dream and about doing something for myself. It was exciting, and I felt as if I had the best secret ever. I would tell no one because I knew that the reasons *not* to do it would outnumber the reasons to do it. I knew the doubting eyes would appear and all the reasons of why I couldn't would forever be engraved in my mind.

> *Have you ever dreamed of WHO you want to be? Start Dreaming!*

I remember sitting down across from this woman who didn't know me. She didn't know the struggles of my life. She didn't see the broken woman wishing for her dream to come true. She didn't know how much this meant to me. And she didn't know how much this meant God in me finding my way. But I was there and as I began to talk, I realized that this was something that I longed for more than I realized. For years—I'm talking over sixteen years—I had wanted to go to school. To be a teacher was placed in my heart and never left.

Have you ever had a dream, a thought or image of who you want to become but it was just never a good time? You found that all the reasons *not* to pursue it outweighed why you should? It had never been a good time for me. Whether it was finances, time, or family needs, I always put aside my desires to be available to support everyone else in their endeavors, in their dreams and in their busy schedules. I felt that it was never my time and that it was over, too late and never a possibility. I was forty-five—life over—right? So this was it... This was my time. And, no one knew I was there, which was exciting! It was just me, God and this lady who held my future in her hands.

As I began to talk about my dreams of what I wanted to do with MY life, I began to realize that I mattered; what I did would mean something. My family never made me feel like I didn't, but I realized that I always felt that what I did for MY life didn't really make a difference. But in this moment, it did. I began to sit taller in the chair, as if standing up for myself and what I wanted to accomplish was important.

As we finished up our conversation, she asked me if I was ready and did I need to call anyone. I sat there, unable to respond or move. All the scenarios flashed through my mind, the "what if's" felt like cement blocks on my feet and I only responded, "No, there is no one I want to call and yes, I'm ready."

She slapped her hands on her desk, stood up and said, "Let's do this!" She startled me when she did that and I think she was almost as excited as I was. The steps walking over to the registration building were the longest steps I've ever walked. The parking lot seemed to be endless on this quest for my very own redemption and it was only a football stadium away. What if someone saw me and talked me out of it? I mean, how was I going to tell my husband, my children, and my friends and family that I would not be available for their every need at the moment they needed it? How was I, in the worst time financially, going to tell my husband I would find a new job that was flexible and that would mean less income? How was I going to do this?! But it didn't seem to matter at the moment. In this one decision, I had just changed the course of my life, jumping in feet-first in finding my purpose and saying yes. Free- falling into faith is what I equate it to. My sixteen- year detour

> *Every day you are one decision away from changing your life.*

led me back to my path, and I was finally moving in a forward direction. Every day you are one decision away from changing it.

I just have to think that there are many women out there sitting where I was; thinking it's too late. If I had stood still in that one moment with that clipping in hand, shoving it in my pocket, I would have regretted it. Time still would have moved forward whether I had done it or not. And that was what I was thinking about. So I registered that day, and I sat in my car for the longest time afterward. I couldn't believe what I had just done.

I did it; I stood up for myself; I stood up for my life and we—God and me—took control of the future He had for me and we would do the unimaginable. As I drove home, the strength began to pour into me. The confidence I felt in taking back my life and accomplishing what I felt was fulfilling. As I told my husband, his reaction was of concern. He had known that I had wanted to do this for a very long time, but how were we going to do this. The woman had talked to me about scholarships, grants and other resources that I could pull from and I would just have to trust in the one and only God who I knew had put me here. I believe that if you have a thought or idea about your life that never goes away, it's a calling and you need to explore it. It might just be a piece of your purpose. So I began my four and half year journey that day.

It was my first semester, and the class was English Comp I. I was not excited and the subject seemed intimidating. I announced on the first day of class that I was not a writer. My professor smiled and said, "We'll see about that." Over time, I came to love writing! I became obsessed with it. At the end of the semester we were given topics and had to write a final essay. But there was a bonus. One topic was about your "Pursuit of Happiness" and it was a contest in the whole college. There would be three winners and they could attend a John Maxwell conference with Chris Gardner who was the inspiration for the movie. The three winners could go to the conference, and have lunch as well with all that were invited. I looked over the topics and thought this one was the one for me. Look at me, sitting in college classes to be a teacher. A woman now in her mid-forties, who has been searching for her happiness and purpose, who now is taking steps in fulfilling her dream after sixteen years of living in "the waiting period." The topic seemed effortless.

So I began to write and… you guessed it. I won third place! What?! I attended the conference, met Chris Gardner and sat next to the president of the college while he read my essay. Over the course of the remaining years, as I requested scholarships, they were always there. There were a few times that I was about to cancel a class, because that was the deal I had made with my husband. I would not take any class if the funds weren't there. But just as I was canceling, a check would arrive or a scholarship would be applied. At this point my husband began to scratch his head as the miracles or a "that was a weird moment" became clear; it's a God thing.

I graduated and then transferred to the university and began my final two years of becoming a teacher. I still couldn't believe I was doing it. What I have found is that the road less travelled, although difficult, was well worth it. The late night essays, the group discussions and testing became a way of life, but it was necessary to push through this season. This will definitely go in the books as being one of my greatest accomplishments. This pursuit wasn't just about getting a degree. It was about setting guidelines for my future and gaining the confidence I needed. I was willing to put in the time and He, without a doubt, poured on a little grace to aid my effort. There were moments that were hard, but I was constantly reminded that the cross was hard. Reality would set in and I'd pull up my big-girl pants and press on.

> *Believe that those valley moments are game changers.*

After I was three years in, the part-time schooling turned into full-time. The requirements of my degree had me in a classroom all day student teaching for a semester, which was not going to work with my current job. So I had to make a decision about my job status. At this point my husband was on the bandwagon that this college thing was God's path for me, and he supported whatever decision I would make. So I plowed forward and completed the requirements.

Believe that those moments where you just know that although it seems you're going against the grain and it's hard; it's right. Do you recall moments you missed but now see clearly that He was pushing you through? Maybe you need to go back and recapture them. Those moments just might change the course of your life, change your path, or change your heart toward becoming who you are meant to be.

Questions for Your Journey

- What are those moments that you missed but now see His hand guiding you through?

- Who do you want to be? What has He placed in your heart?

CHAPTER 24

Following your dreams.

I continued on to what I thought would be my graduation in the fall of 2015. To be a student teacher I had to pass various state exams. I purchased the study materials, researched extensively and took the exams. I passed all of them with flying colors except one. This was the first time I hadn't passed an exam. Are you kidding me?! Not only did I not pass it the first time, I didn't pass the second time! I came up short of passing by just a few questions. This would postpone my student teaching and my graduation.

I began to question God about this path and wondered if this was it... What in the world was happening? Why wasn't it working? Was this just me taking control and calling it God's will? I was doing everything right—I thought. I questioned God's intentions for my life. Until... in walked the majestic blue heron moments; the moments of Him reminding me of his presence and care for me.

I went out to the beach and had a heated discussion with God about this path He had me on. Was the long journey to becoming a teacher, all the late night studies and papers, all for nothing? Suddenly, amidst my tantrum right there in the sand, in the stillness I heard, "teacher of what?"

"What are you talking about?!" I shouted and threw my hands up. *Are you kidding me?!* I now resembled a child throwing a fit because she didn't get her way.

For those of you who've attended college, it's exhausting. I was a full-time student beginning my senior year, still holding a full-time job, a full-time mother of three, and wife. All I could do was throw myself in the sand and cry like a baby. "What are you talking about? I'm going to be a teacher, a middle school English teacher!" And that was it. Just silence. No explanation, no hint of a sign, nothing. Confused, I went home.

I told my son, the musician, who is so much further in his spiritual walk than I ever dreamed of being, that I felt God ask, "teacher of what?" He just smiled and said, "I don't know." But he did. It was all over his face; he knew and understood what God meant. One of my favorite quotes from Mark Batterson is that, "God doesn't call the qualified, He qualifies the called."

"God does not call the qualified, He qualifies the called."

And so that night, this book began. From the fit at the beach, I came home and started writing my story. I felt a need to understand why He had me travel so far to understand who He wanted me to be. I needed to find Him in my story, in my uglies, in my life so that I could take the next step. In my final semester, I still could not pass that last exam. Unbelievable! Why were these barriers keeping me from the finish line? What about all the financial saves He gave along the way in getting me to this point? I talked with my university counselor and there was a way for me to graduate without my student teaching but would require three more classes. At this point I just wanted to finish.

At the beginning of the semester, I checked my financial obligation. This was usually a zero balance, but this time it showed I had a $533.00 balance due, and that didn't include what I'd need for books. Knowing I didn't have it, I feared the door was closing on graduating.

I prayed about it for days. One morning, I was driving my son to school and he was complaining about having to go. I said, "You have to be there, so just show up. And while you're there, knock it out of the park." At that same moment, a pastor on KLOVE was giving an encouraging word about showing up for your life. How about that timing, right? As I dropped him off, I realized I had to take my own advice. So I went home, got dressed and was determined to go to the university; I would show up. I decided that I would participate in my life and knock it out of the park!

This took me to the final leg of this journey of finding my way. It started with a prayer and solidified to me the power behind prayer.

Questions for Your Journey

- Make a timeline of your history and see how it's influenced you today. Follow your heart for success in your future by using your experiences to guide you.

- Do you have a dream of doing something big (college, career, children, etc.)? What is stopping you and what steps can you take today to make it a reality?

Prayer

"Then you will call on me and come and pray to me, and I will listen."
Jeremiah 29:12

CHAPTER 25

The power behind prayer.

As I sat in my driveway, I prayed. I didn't pray for Him to do this for me. I didn't pray for Him to save me. All I prayed was for Him to be with me. To guide my steps and put the right people in front of me and I'll do the rest. This was me showing up, like I told my son, and this was me knocking it out of the park, right?

I still wasn't confident so as I neared the university I phoned a good friend who understood all the workings of receiving financial aid. She stayed on the phone with me until I ended up in a parking lot I was unfamiliar with. I started at the foundation office and talked with a

[*Trust in the Lord.*]

woman who was helpful but didn't give me any sign of immediate help that I needed. So I exited and stopped in the center of a three-way sidewalk. I looked back from where I had just come. Over to my right was the president's office and to my left and I saw the back of a building. I wasn't sure which way to go but I knew I wasn't leaving until I had accomplished my goal. So I stopped in that circle on the sidewalk and I prayed. Right there, out loud. I lowered my head and asked for Him to guide my steps. Which way do I go? I decided to take a left, to see what the building was. It was the financial aid office and realized I had never seen it from the back.

I had talked with them many times and did not feel confident in what I needed to ask; but today, I decided, was a new day.

As quoted in Proverbs 3:5-6, "Trust in the Lord with all your heart and lean not on your own understanding; in all your ways acknowledge him and he shall direct your paths." So I did just that. I sat and waited for what seemed an eternity amongst all the twenty-somethings all trying to get the same result.

As I heard my name called I began my walk toward what seemed the impossible walk. But what do I have to lose... show up, right? The young person sitting across from me in no way knew the part she would play in what defined the moment of truth for me. She asked how she could help and I began to tell her my story. I was to graduate in the spring; I have three final classes and look at me; I'm getting older every day! She laughed and proceeded to type in to my account. She noticed a scholarship hanging out there and she went to investigate. She came back and asked me these two questions.

"Have you registered to graduate?" I replied, yes. She asked, "Is this your final three classes?" I replied, yes.

She stated that whoever she talked with had agreed to apply the scholarship I had always received each semester but that I would have a $33.00 balance. What?! It was all I could do to hold it together. An uncontrollable-sobbing-almost-fifty-year-old is not who you want to be in the financial aid building at a university. I told her I wasn't or couldn't look at her for a moment because what she just did for me was life-changing.

Have you ever had that moment of reckoning when you realized your steps were numbered and assigned with His grace all over them? The loving hand, extended out to me that day will forever be etched in my mind. The moments, minutes and hours leading up to this one moment, in the car talking to my child about showing up and knocking it out of the park! This was it. This was a home run for me that day that also led me to here... writing this. This meant that I would graduate, that it would be finished. But that wasn't the end that day.

She then asked how I was to pay for books. It was hundreds of dollars for these three books and all my classes were requiring it. She mentioned across campus was a "borrow a book" program and maybe they would have one of my books. So I trekked my way across campus and found the building. I entered and found no one. There were a few students milling around but no one to ask about the program. As I was leaving, I noticed a light shining at the end of one corridor. I peeked inside and there was a woman with a smile from ear to ear. I asked about the program and we began to talk. As we talked, I realized we had similar paths in life and felt an instant connection. She encouraged me to go a community computer and she would email me the link. I would then search for the book and the policy was that they would lend me one of the books to use. That was great! God's little bonuses amid turmoil; I'll take it.

I searched, but it listed none of my books. Not a one. So I stuck my head in and thanked her for her time. She asked if she could look for me and I waited... hoping I had done it wrong.

But, she shook her head and said, "We'll have to call it done." I agreed and thanked her. She said, "No, we're calling this done." As I strained to see if she was kidding, she announced that she would order the books, all three of them! I stood there speechless, and I started to cry at this point and I asked her why she would do this for me. When I first met her, I had told her that this was my final chapter of my journey, of doing what God had planned for me and these books were necessary in order for me to graduate. This is what you call sharing your story, giving your testimony. She stated that she wanted to be a part of my story and part of His plan in my life. Hallelujah!

What I found through this process is that when you share your life, share your stories and share your heart, people respond. That's what we do, that is what God calls us to do. In Hebrews 10:24-25, "And let us consider how we may spur one another on toward love and good deeds, not giving up meeting together, as some are in the habit of doing, but encouraging one another—and all the more as you see the Day approaching."

My prayer from earlier that morning came back to me... I prayed for Him to guide my steps, to place people in front of me and that I would do the rest. And that He did. As I exited the building and walked to my car, I felt as if I was floating. I wanted to fist pump and do that moon walk thing across the parking lot, but it would mortify my boys. How could this be that today, when what seemed impossible, wasn't? Nothing is impossible with Christ at the forefront of your life! I have seen that over and over in my life.

But Jesus looked at them and said, "With man this is impossible, but with God all things are possible." Matthew 19:26.

I sat in my car and screamed "YOU ARE AMAZING!" He is amazing… has over-the-top love for you and me. With Him and through Him there is no fear. By having faith and believing you can do anything, you can and you will. Changing your attitude can change your day, which can change your life. When you put all your eggs in... Push all your chips to the center of whatever it is you're going through, He will provide, if it is His will for your life.

Changing your attitude can change your day, which can change your life.

Mark 11:24 says, "Therefore I tell you, whatever you ask for in prayer, believe that you have received it, and it will be yours." But you will never know if you don't step out, participate, show up and watch God go! Have faith in His plans and be all-in.

I completed my education; I graduated with honors and validated those donors who believed in me. Walking across the stage that day was a culmination of everything leading up to that one moment of truth. To my family, my friends, the donors, the strangers who played very specific roles, but most of all, to God, I thank you.

He extends a hand to all of us, and living out our faith in response can reflect His great love for others. When others see the decisions you make, watch the way you live your life, and say yes to Him, He is pleased.

I had taken a picture of myself on the way to the university that day when I first showed up. This is what my post was on social media:

> *"This is me on my way to UWF today in what I call "showing up." I heard on KLOVE today that in order for God to do His work, you have to show up. Participate in your fate. I started my day stressed but decided to show up and let Him do His will. But before I started out on my venture, I prayed. Not for Him to make it all work out but to just be with me. To guide my steps and to put the people in front of me I needed and I would do the rest. In getting out of my car was the*

> *first step in doing my part of the miracles He had in store for me today. There have been many throughout this four-year journey to teach. I left in awe of His grace and mercy today and this day goes down in the books for me. So the moral of my story today... get out of the car and show up... it's not over until the big guy says so. Be present and watch Him work."*

That's what I call "showing up." It all began four years prior. I had always wanted to teach but never had more than a high school education. I had spent my entire life doing just what everyone else wanted me to do. I always strived to be the best daughter, wife and mother, but couldn't shake the longing to be educated. A teacher was all I ever wanted to be. I was in my final year of college and I was tired when He said "teacher of what?" After this experience of Him guiding my steps, showing up in the road with wings like an angel, carrying me across the finish line, I now understand His "teacher of what" response. While reading through Scriptures on never giving up, I came across this one in 1 Corinthians 9:24-27 that resonated with me.

[*Show up for your life.*]

"Do you not know that in a race all the runners run, but only one gets the prize? Run in such a way as to get the prize. Everyone who competes in the games goes into strict training. They do it to get a crown that will not last, but we do it to get a crown that will last forever. Therefore I do not run like someone running aimlessly; I do not fight like a boxer beating the air. No, I strike a blow to my body and make it my slave so that after I have preached to others, I myself will not be disqualified for the prize."

Although these moments in life can seem like the end at the time, it is only an end in that season. You may believe that there is something so much better down the road, but first you have to get *on* the road. If the God I know took the time to re-route, walk through and show up for me when needed, I know He is doing this for you.

Being present means being still in His presence. It is in the quiet still moments or the "stillness" that He meets us because that is when He has our undivided attention. But there are other times He meets us in the chaos and that is where, amidst it all, we just need to breathe and trust. He will do astounding things in your life if you just believe. So love yourself, love your neighbor and move forward. Don't get discouraged by the detours; embrace them, learn from them and keep moving forward. God only knows where I would be without them.

Being still in His presence is where He meets us.

I could have taken that news clipping and tossed it aside and said, "If only." But I took the long and treacherous road to believing in the path He had for me. Was it easy? No. Was it hard? Yes. Was it worth it? Absolutely! Those are the moments or valleys where we grow the most. Sometimes they are to strengthen us, to give us a boldness that only true warriors of Christ know. Be confident in your stride and testify when those divine appointments arise. I know my path today—tomorrow, maybe not. But being intentional and never underestimating the power of prayer keeps me going in the right direction.

Questions for Your Journey

❖ What is something that you know will be hard but you feel led to do anyway?

❖ Take the time to list out what your heart has been telling you to do and make it happen!

CHAPTER 26

Forgiveness is hard.

I would assume that most of us have issues with forgiveness. It's a simple act, right? Simple, but not easy. In my life there have been many reasons *not* to forgive others and I've held on to my suffering for years, keeping it alive and active within my soul. I have worn the anger like a suit of armor that I swore I would never take off. I'll show them, right? As I've read about forgiving others, though, I've come to realize that the offender is not who I'm punishing by withholding forgiveness. Forgiveness is best for the one extending it because it releases you from the bondage of whatever pain that person has caused. Not forgiving holds you hostage to the hurt, keeps you from trusting others, and experiencing true peace. I've read that there are stages of forgiveness and that we have to go through them in order to get satisfaction in the freedom it provides. There are so many reasons to forgive and yet we still find it hard to do.

So, in order for us to relate to the word "forgiveness," let's take a closer look. As I examined the meaning, I found that it requires a response on our part. It's an action or process of "a release of guilt to another." What I found most interesting are the synonyms of forgiveness. Examples are: pardon, clemency, and absolution, all demonstrating a willingness to show compassion to the other. But the one word I most rest on is the word "mercy." It is all throughout the Bible, where Jesus reminds us how important forgiveness is.

The verse most referenced is that of Jesus on the cross, where he says, "Father forgive them; for they do not know what they are doing" found in Luke 23:24.

I am reminded of the mercy given to me throughout my life. We've all experienced this great show of love and compassion, even when we didn't deserve it. To deliver mercy means showing compassion, even when you have the power to punish or harm others for their actions. But by not forgiving, are we harming them or us? Just as we make the wrong choices and ask for forgiveness, we expect God to show this great mercy toward us.

Words that are similar are: grace, blessing, godsend and showing favor, with the opposite being ruthlessness and cruelty. By forgiving, we show mercy to others when they do not deserve it. I am not saying to condone their actions, but focusing on mercy indicates we understand what it means to forgive. It's incredibly hard, friends, but necessary in order for us to move forward.

The Bible commands us to forgive. Matthew 6:14-15 reads, "For if you forgive others their trespasses, your heavenly Father will also forgive you, but if you do not forgive others their trespasses, neither will your Father forgive your trespasses."

Forgiveness is a willful act that is intentional and a choice. A choice made by us but also by God. I have held on to anger for years with fear riding on its coattails because of the "what ifs?" What if I forgive and they feel like they got away with it? What if I forgive and they feel like they won? What if I forgive and I can't get past it? But, what if you forgave and it made you happy? What if you forgave and it set you free? What if you forgave and life mattered again? Forgiving others is an action that releases YOU from bondage; not them. They haven't gotten away with anything and they haven't won. They will have their own cross to bear, but you sweet friend, have a life worth living.

[*Forgiveness is intentional.*]

When I finally began to understand forgiveness it led me to a space of tranquil peace. Not that I understood everything God was doing in my journey, but He revealed Himself to me in the moments spent with Him.

Sometimes my moments with Him are intentionally planned and look like typical "quiet times" (prayer, Bible reading, etc.). But other times occur unexpectedly when He shows up unannounced and I feel fear because I don't understand what He's trying to do in my life.

Such as the day when I asked Him one simple question, "Is this it; is this the end?" And His answer forever changed me.

Questions for Your Journey

- What if you closed your eyes and went on gut and intuition? Where would you go and what would you do? Do it!

- What prayer do you need to pray?

- Who do you need to forgive? Forgiveness will set you free!

UNDERSTANDING

"For it is by grace you have been saved, through faith – and this is not from yourselves, it is the gift of God – not by works, so that no one can boast. For we are God's handiwork, created in Christ Jesus to do good works, which God prepared in advance for us to do."
~ Ephesians 2:8-10

CHAPTER 27

Expect the unexpected.

So why is it when you feel as if you're headed in the right direction you hit a wall? A place where you stop and wonder, is this it? Well, this is where I was. Having finished this book and edited it twenty thousand times, something happened that rocked my world and forced me to put it down and take a break.

Over the past months, I've gone back and forth about whether I wanted to share this pretty big save. Once I decided to include it here, I wondered why I even questioned sharing it in the first place.

The event was totally unexpected and I had no idea when I awoke that day that it was going to take a turn for the worse. So here goes, one last "save" for the books, hoping to reach someone out there contemplating suicide.

I'm in tears just writing the word suicide again. But this time was different; this time was pure evil. I'm embarrassed, confused and altogether terrified to reveal this ugliness. It's a moment in time that I felt the trimmers of Satan himself and God in the battle of my life. So here goes, here's to not wasting a save.

> [*Kick back when your spirit is challenged.*]

Six months ago I was in an accident, a biking accident that changed my life. Let me set the stage. It was a typical morning; I was out for a ride and, having reached my turn-around point, I headed home. The road bike and I had reached a good speed and my head was down and focused, contemplating my morning and getting back in time for carpool. Having been in prayer just moments prior, I had just said to God that I would go to the ends of the earth for His good, for His glory and how I was up to the challenge. Little did I know, just down the road I was to be challenged not only physically, but also spiritually; yes, once again. Friends, when you are in love with Jesus, Satan will not stop. He will whisper in your ear, and will always be at your back. He prowls around seeking who to destroy. It is up to you when in spiritual warfare to kick back.

When traveling on a road bike, your speed is quick and your focus is much more in tune with your surroundings because of this. As I was passing cars parked to my right, I saw a flash of movement from the corner of my eye. Enter now the dog.

This was not a small dog; this was a large bulldog/boxer built like a brick house. It happened so fast that I did not even have time to brake. All I could hear was the sound of his nails digging into the concrete and the impact of him colliding with my bike. All I could feel was how much air I caught as the impact threw me and my bike up and flipped over. Luckily, I wear a helmet, but once you're midair, all you can think about is the hurt that's coming. It all happened so fast. I just remember landing on the right side of my head with two hard hits and the sound of my body and bike smacking down and sliding on the pavement. I remember screaming and crying as the dog circled around me. I still hear those sounds and cringe to this day.

I'm sure many of you have had accidents that, when you reflect on them, bring back memories you want to forget. Why do our minds hold so tightly to these moments and not let us move past them? Those painful memories help to create the walls in your heart that hold you hostage.

At the time I did not know what the dog was going to do, but I was rendered motionless from the impact. As I lay in the road cradling my head, I could hear people coming and stopping to help. There were so many questions; I answered the best I could. But during of all of this, I began to shut down and although I could hear their questions, I couldn't respond. I was answering them in my head, but I realized I could not speak. My other senses were heightened, though. The sky became so blue and the clouds were so fluffy and moving so fast. The noise of the people and cars disappeared and all I could hear was the rustling, yet peaceful breeze. I was aware of everything going on around me, but I wasn't able to participate.

Then the dreaded question popped into my head... "Is this it...? Is this the end?" I was so terrified in that moment of all the things I hadn't done; all the things I hadn't said. All the "saves" I had wasted. In that moment, all I wanted was a chance to get it right.

I prayed, "Please don't let this be it" and just as I began to close my eyes, I felt a slap on my face and it was as if someone turned the volume up. Suddenly, all the loud sounds, conversations, gurneys and questions came roaring back. I was loaded into the ambulance and taken away for treatment of my head injury.

Since that day I haven't been the same. I experienced vertigo at first—as in walking into walls, tripping over furniture and trying to appear normal while in conversation, but feeling like I was spinning out of control. Now the moments of unsteadiness and dizziness are less frequent and occur at random moments in my day, but they still come.

To expect the unexpected is to be prepared for what comes your way. But the moment that I want to talk about is when I experienced a battle—of life or death—where I was the bystander on the sidelines watching to see who would win.

CHAPTER 28

What's it going to be?

We all have the daily struggles of not feeling good enough or worthy enough to get through one day and into the next. I had become so depressed, unmotivated, and pitiful that I'm embarrassed to say this was me. I went to work each day; I made dinner each day; I drove the children to school each day, but I was just going through the motions with no real purpose. I felt motivated to make things happen in my life, but I couldn't seem to get beyond the starting block. My mind was all over the place and it took everything I had to just make it to bed at night.

The two days leading up until this day I want to share with you, I had a terrible headache, and I lay in bed and slept for most of them. On the third day, which was a Wednesday, I woke up sobbing. I just couldn't take it anymore and I just wanted my head to stop bothering me. I wanted the feelings of sorrow to go away and I felt lower than I've ever felt in my life—a place where your face is pressed against the bottom of nowhere. That's where I was.

My husband had worked from home that day and I have to say, it was a blessing. He was trying to comfort me but I just needed to get away and found myself in my shop crumpled in a ball on the floor. I was out of control and was not sure what was happening. My husband had to leave, and I assured him I was fine. But after he left things changed and I felt calm. It was an eerie calm that made me feel as if I was not there. This was not like anything I've ever experienced.

So I did the most horrific thing a person can ever do—I walked upstairs with a knife, sat in the shower, and attempted to end my life. There, I said it.

The day was December 13, and I will forever think of this day as the day we won the war. I was so disappointed in myself. I do not know what happened. The person I am now was saying, "Girl, get up!" But I was so far removed that it was impossible to hear her. It's hard to explain and I hope to never be in that place again. That was not my plan when I woke up that morning and obviously I didn't go through with it. My husband came home and shook me out of my haze and the brutal internal verbal attacks that I was experiencing.

But during those moments, I saw and felt the hatred of Satan, the element of fear at its highest and the overwhelming battle I was in. At the same time, I also felt the love of God, the power of His right hand pulling my heart toward Him and it was then that I knew I was not alone. I felt the tug on my heart and I heard the opposite of everything Satan was saying to me about who I am. I don't know where I would be if I hadn't had that love to snatch me out of such a violent experience, but I did. He threw me another save.

I don't want to dwell on my suicide attempt for long. But I share it to communicate that I understand the feeling of lost hope, unworthiness and being stuck in a bottomless pit of helplessness from which there seems to be no escape. It is my hope that if you are ever in a battle that requires you to fight with everything you have, you are aware that He also stands beside you in these battles. I hope you listen to the words of love, the words of confirmation that you *are* worth it, even when ending it seems a much better offer. I pray that you believe in His love for you, you stand on faith and never, ever let the enemy have victory over your life, your story, your song.

He stands beside you in your battles.

So after you've survived and come out of a moment like this, what do you do? For me—I plan.

CHAPTER 29

Are you a strategic planner?

So how should we handle such experiences and get on with life? I was fortunate to have been rescued and I know this. But it doesn't take away the fact that I am worried beyond belief that I could have another day like that where I was on the verge of ending it all. I'm a planner though, and we planners prepare ahead of time.

The job of the manager of any household is to plan for what's coming, to stay one step ahead. In reading thru Scripture, there were many great planners in the Bible's history. Strategic planning was not only a concept throughout the Bible, but it was also something that God commanded or mandated from people in order for Him to work through them. This led me to get a tattoo. Let me clarify— God did not *tell* me to get a tattoo— I'm not claiming that, but I felt like it would help me to remember. I'm saying this lightheartedly, so please don't judge. But for my struggle with worry about the past reoccurring, it was a permanent reminder of "whose" I am. A branding, so to speak; Yes, I'm going with that.

The men in the Word that were strategic planners all left their mark in moments of greatness that expanded the kingdom. They included Moses, Joshua, Nehemiah, David, Jesus, and Paul and it was through the great acts of these men and their well laid-plans that God did amazing things. Moses planned and was a strategic thinker when he sent spies into the land of Canaan. In Joshua 6, a strategic plan

[*Plan ahead and be ready for battle.*]

was in place to lead the Israelites into the Promise Land. In the story of Nehemiah, the plan was in the reconstruction of the walls of Jerusalem. David was a strategic thinker even as a teenager during the win over Goliath. And as a man, David brought that planning into battle where God gave him great victory.

Jesus was the son of God, the ultimate planner, more strategic than most. He recruited leaders, equipped them, and sent them out to do His work. His greatest strategy was in his teaching, performing miracles and understanding what the cross meant to all of humanity. And Paul was a great planner of the early church, setting his eyes on the cities of great numbers and seeing the influence he could have.

These men were strategic thinkers and planners in God's world and they all accomplished His work. They planned, but always gave their plans over to God's will. It is written in Proverbs 19:21, "Many are the plans in a man's heart, but it is the Lord's purpose that prevails." God clarifies that it is not our life, our plan or our own thoughts that are of importance. It continues in Proverbs 16:9, with one of my favorites that, "In his heart a man plans his course, but the Lord determines his steps."

So what does this have to do with me and where I am? For me I got a tattoo. I did not just think about it one day and do it. It came to me in a dream and the next six days I became focused and I planned and contemplated my next move.

Have you ever been given a thought or an idea and it takes on the speed of a freight train? It's all you think about but you tell no one. It's a thought that you know family, friends, and anyone who knows you may question your rationale. Well, for me the struggle with vertigo and the two-sided battle in the shower was taking its toll. Sometimes certain decisions in your life need only your attention and God's. I rarely feel the need to discuss everything with my husband or family. Most of the time, we tend to do what's best for the whole family and move on. For this decision I knew I might get some pushback, but something kept pressing me to explore it.

Heaven stands in your fear.

I find it is in those times of fear and despair that God and Heaven are closest. They stand for our fear by giving us their strength; they stand in our despair by giving us hope, and they stand when we're afraid of showing who is boss. They stand for everyone with love, peace, and authority. And that is where I found myself the Sunday morning after having a dream of a tattoo on my right wrist.

I was restless and worried about not being able to control my thoughts or actions. It was keeping me from getting on with my life and I knew I needed a sign of something to remind me who was in control. So it was this dream that started me on this journey of "Grace." The marking I ended up getting reminds me daily that His grace is enough and it is by His right hand that I do His work. It says in Isaiah 41:10 "Don't worry, because I am with you. Don't be afraid, because I am your God. I will make you strong and will help you; I will support you with my right hand that saves you." I'm not saying you have to get a tattoo to feel this empowerment but for me, I did. So early one Sunday morning….

Now, before I go any further, just know this about me: I am a type-A personality. I'm one who needs at least 3-5 signs that I'm heading in the right direction, just to be sure. God gets creative but I believe He had a little fun with me this time. I'm sure I can be altogether exhausting, but He humors me and chases me down each time until I get it right.

When my alarm went off that morning, I was in the middle of a dream where I was sporting a new tattoo. I thought, weird, but I shrugged it off and got ready for work at the church. Now the strange thing is that I never remember my dreams—ever. So this was eventful, and it was a moment that would lead me to the chair six days later. So, remembering my dream would be sign #1.

That same day while at work, a beautiful friend of mine approached me. Now, you know those people who seem to bring the love and presence of God with them when they walk in the door? The ones where the Holy Spirit oozes from them… this is that lady. She said to me, "Look at my foot." I looked at her and looked down and to my surprise, she had gotten a tattoo. I was taken back. If this woman got a tattoo, well then maybe it wasn't too crazy for me. I told her about my dream the night before and she asked what the tattoo was a picture of. But that was the problem; I couldn't remember. Now, this I know, it was on my right wrist and was a single word but I did not understand what it said. She said to pray on it and in good time He would reveal the word. So my friend, who I hold in such high regard, had gotten a tattoo that would be sign #2.

Now doing what I do well, I told no one. I am a constant surprise! But as a planner, I had to research what it meant to get a tattoo. How permanent is it? Is it a sin? Is there a difference between a Christian tattoo and a non-Christian tattoo? What does the Bible say about tattoos? Is there a difference in the pain level depending on what body part you get the tattoo? Can I die from a tattoo? I searched everything I could and what I came up with was good information.

What I found was interesting. I felt confident it was going to be permanent, and it would hurt no matter what. After reading about whether it was a sin or not, I felt confident that, as long as the content wasn't dishonoring to God and I was expressing myself in a positive way, it's not a moral issue, just a personal preference. And no—death is not the result of getting a tattoo.

So, Monday I headed into town to run a few errands. While shopping, I glanced at all the merchandise. By the time I got to the front of the store, the word to imprint on my arm became clear. I waited in line at the register for a bit but I had to go back and look at something that had triggered the word. Halfway back through the store, on the bottom shelf was a little wooden sign that read, "Your Grace is enough." "Grace." Was that it? I took a picture of the sign and went about my day—Sign #3.

[*His Grace is enough!*]

The songs on the radio that day were grace-themed. It became comical how often I heard it—Sign #4. That word resonated with me throughout the day and as I looked around my home and office, I began to realize that I had that word on many decorative crosses without knowing it. The word was surrounding me—Sign #5.

So what is it about signs? Are they premonitions? A premonition is a hunch, a feeling that something may happen. Whether good or bad, it's an anticipation of something to come. And that's what I had. But as I'm writing today, I do not think this premonition was me getting a tattoo. My tattoo represents the strategic planning in the process of my premonition of things to come. There are ninety-five Bible verses that speak of feelings of premonitions. This is not the same as prophesying or divination; those words are altogether different than what happened to me. I was praying and taking this dream to God and asking Him what it meant, what I was to do with it and *was I getting a tattoo*?

On day four I got a random call from an unknown number. When my husband asked who it was, I just shook my head and said, "That's interesting." The number was from ***Grace***ville, Florida. And they didn't just call once; they called back the next day, too. I know no one from Graceville, nor did I even know it existed. Sooo—Sign #6. All right, I'm in!

The next two days I talked a lot to my friend about her tattoo and my tattoo and she insisted on coming with me to be a part of this moment. Friday night we rolled up to the tattoo parlor and I reflected on the events of the past week which led me there. If only my family could see me now! It all seemed impossible—from the dream, the sign in the store, the songs on the radio, the crosses surrounding me with the word grace, and the random calls from Graceville—all leading me to be sitting on a leather sofa, watching an episode of *Cheers* about tattoos, waiting for my turn. It was reminders that I am not alone. My word was Grace, with no hesitation. And in the middle of my grace is a cross as a reminder to me that I am His.

I went back and purchased that little wooden sign and it sits on my mantel as a reminder of his nudge that day. His grace is enough; of course it is. Another word that became significant for me is the name Anna. At the end of my sophomore year in college, I attended a spiritual walk, and during that weekend God placed me right where He wanted me. Each group of women sat at a table that had a name of a woman from the Bible. I sat at the table of Anna. I knew nothing about Anna. I didn't think much of it until now, five years later, right now in this moment as I write.

I found out that she was in the book of Luke three times. They described her as an old woman who married and lived with her husband for seven years and then was widowed for over eighty-four years. She was a disciplined woman who prayed and fasted, never leaving the temple. I wanted to connect with this woman in some way. Why was I at her table? Well, here I sit, in my final editing and this spiritual walk weekend and Anna comes to mind. I looked her up again and read the same information I had read before. I then looked up the meaning behind the name Anna and sat there in amazement as everything became linked together. I'm sure this was a moment in Heaven where they all were sitting on the edge of their seats with God shushing them and saying, "Wait for it, wait for it, here it comes!" Are you ready?

The name Anna means *Grace*. He sat me at the table of grace. I am sitting here with my hand over mouth in astonishment that my God would think that much of me and give me this much.

So the word grace has surrounded me for years. And as I looked around, I saw all the crosses that display the word "Grace" and knew that all along He was covering me in it. I don't know if I would have tied all this together if I hadn't written this book. If I had not written a timeline, journaled my thoughts, recognized my moments of grace, my moments of mercy; I would have missed it.

In your life, throughout your days, in your smallest and final moments of each situation where He stitches it all together to create a masterpiece called "you," just be open to it. He covers you in the midst of the battles and valleys, on the fringes of hope, where He stands for you and gives you strength and hope to have faith. Now as a constant reminder on my right wrist, the hand that leads me, His right hand, not only reads "Grace," but He has marked me with a cross in His grace.

You don't have to have a tattoo to know this. He was ever so patient waiting for the moment when I would finally put all the pieces together and knows that He is here with me always. I'm sure He's relieved that my understanding has come full circle. He sat me at the table of grace, friends! All is done by His grace alone and whatever the future holds, please always remember that His Grace is enough.

QUESTIONS FOR YOUR JOURNEY

- ❖ Describe a time where the unexpected happened and you were sucker-punched?

- ❖ Describe a time when Heaven stood in your fear.

- ❖ What is your word that He speaks over you?

Blessed

So do not fear, for I am with you; do not be dismayed,
for I am your God. I will strengthen you and help you;
I will uphold you with my righteous right hand.
Isaiah 41:10

CHAPTER 30

Sitting in it.

So here we are… at the end of my journey and I am feeling blessed. I threw a lot at you and hopefully walked you through some of your detours in finding the beauty of grace and mercy. This journey is not over. He continues to lead me into this new chapter of what I call "sitting in it." I've been sitting in it for a while now and I feel as if I'm ready to move. Through this faith journey, I have a greater understanding of who I am, what role God plays in my life and what true and fierce faith is. I started this journey of writing this in hopes of finding God in my life. I wanted to understand the meaning behind the love of God.

It means loving at all costs, no matter what. It recognizes that the small things are the life-changers. It means moving forward when you want to stop. And it's standing up when you want to sit down. It's what I call "free falling" or "falling upward" in his grace and mercy and being open to whatever He's got planned. It's being intentional to walk to the edge of uncertainty, pushing through the fear and trusting that He's got you until the very end.

Jump off; God is good, this I know. He has loved me, as I know He loves you. To walk through a life with Christ is not the easy path, but the path well worth the walk. Showing up for your life is the easy part; it's getting out of your comfort zone that's the hard part. Having real and raw faith amidst the battles, the valleys, and the impossible moment's means knowing God is refining us for something so much better. It's saying "thank you for choosing me to walk with and taking time to refine me for the next leg of the journey." It's knowing that He sees us standing in the road even when we feel alone. It's looking up and reaching out when you can't see what's ahead. It's knowing and believing in something so much bigger than you.

I hope you saw yourself in these chapters and realize that even as far back as the very beginning, people and situations were still the same as they are today. We all have our messes, misses and all need love. I hope that you connected and could dive deep into reflection through my questions, that they helped you see and recognize hope. As you move through your life, I hope that snippets of my story and those in the Bible remind you that you are not alone, especially in those valley moments. Remember that you've got this, and that nothing is impossible in the middle of His grace.

My words for you are these. Don't waste a save. Be fierce in your faith and tell someone about it. *He is counting on you and me* to share our stories, our journeys, and even our messes, to extend a hand to someone else. And please never think your life is a failure, insignificant or that it does not matter. Every moment matters in His eyes and it's what you do with it that is important. He has designed you for His purpose alone, and that is the Creator of this universe waiting for you to acknowledge Him in the room. He loves you more than you can ever imagine and expresses it by extending a hand through grace and giving mercy for the detours you've chosen. Helen Keller's quote of, "A bend in the road is not the end of the road unless you fail to make the turn" is one worth remembering. The bend does not have to be the end, so make the turn and take the opportunities that come your way; they just might be His detour or life-savers for you. I hope that through just a few of my messes, or misses, you could connect and discover those moments in *your* life where you can see God's saves, and gain a better understanding of who you are and who you are meant to be.

So in the defining moments of truth, remember to push through the fear, believe you can and you will, stand up when you want to sit down and never let anyone tell you who you are. You are who He says you are. And that, my sweet friends, is a wonderfully made child of God.

THINGS TO REMEMBER...

We are refined in the valleys.

He walks with us through it.

He still hasn't changed His mind in loving you.

Find faith in the valley moments.

It is by faith that you can stare down fear by proclaiming the name of the Lord.

It is the gathering of stones and our faith that life changes.

He prepares your path for moments in your future.

God finds us and always extends a hand.

God is the only one who can deliver hope.

Inviting God into your marriage is like an anchor that holds you steady in the rough waters.

God is in the room.

When life gets hard, stand up when you want to sit down.

God was pleased!

Believe you can and you will!

Praise Him in your storm. Praise Him FOR your storm.

Having a relationship with God changes your life.

Being in the presence of God is being in the stillness.

The .2 is the hardest than the whole of a marathon.

Quitting would be easy.

His perfect love will always override anything that you feel defeats you.

Living life in the final bursts are life changers.

He sees little 'ole you standing in the road.

Be the light for someone else.

What happens if you don't get what you want?

Begin to be who you want to be and you will eventually ***become*** *the person you are meant to be.*

Opportunity is normally accompanied with a fellow named "fear".

What fires you up? What keeps you up at night? What are your gifts and talents?

"A bend in the road is not the end of the road unless you fail to make the turn." Helen Keller

Fear has nothing to do with God.

His pace is always in stride with yours and He never leaves your side.

What if your detour had to do with someone else in changing their course?

At times, it is the smallest moments that are the most impactful.

Have you ever dreamed of WHO you want to be?
Start Dreaming!

Every day you are one decision away from changing your life.

Believe that those valley moments are game changers.

"God does not call the qualified, He qualifies the called." Mark Batterson

Trust in the Lord.

Changing your attitude can change your day, which can change your life.

Show up for your life.

Being still in His presence is where He meets us.

Forgiveness is intentional.

Kick back when your spirit is challenged.

He stands beside you in your battles.

Plan ahead and be ready for battle.

Heaven stands in your fear.

~ And always remember…

His Grace is enough!

REFERENCES

Holy Bible: New International Version. Zondervan, 2017.

"Dictionary by Merriam-Webster: America's Most-Trusted Online Dictionary." *Merriam-Webster*, Merriam-Webster, www.merriam-webster.com/.

"Meaning of Numbers in the Bible The Number 5." *Meaning of the Number 5 in the Bible*, www.biblestudy.org/bibleref/meaning-of-numbers-in-bible/5.html.

Printed in the United States
By Bookmasters